SERMONS
On United Methodist Beliefs

SERMONS
On United Methodist Beliefs

Kenneth L. Carder

Abingdon Press
Nashville

SERMONS ON UNITED METHODIST BELIEFS

Carder, Kenneth L., 1940-
    Sermons on United Methodist beliefs / Kenneth L. Carder.
       p. cm.
    Includes bibliographical references.
    ISBN 0-687-33864-6 (alk. paper)
    1. United Methodist Church (U.S.)—Sermons. 2. Methodist Church—Sermons. 3. Sermons, American. I. Title.
BX8333.C283S47 1991
252'.076—dc20   90-20144
                                                                      CIP

MANUFACTURED IN THE UNITED STATES OF AMERICA

*To Linda, Sheri, and Sandra, through whom
I perpetually experience Transcendent Grace;
and to Allen and Edith Carder, who quietly exhibit
"holiness and happiness."*

Acknowledgments

When Bishop Sheldon Deucker called to ask if I would be willing to write *Doctrinal Standards and Our Theological Task: Leader's Guide*, I was honored that the Council of Bishops would trust me with such an important assignment, but I was humbled by the enormity of the responsibility. During the subsequent weeks, I lived with the sermons, letters, and other writings of John Wesley. As I immersed myself in Wesley's thought and the doctrinal/theological statement adopted by the 1988 General Conference, I became aware in new ways of the richness of our doctrinal/theological heritage. The Council of Bishops invited me to perform a task, but in reality they gave me a gift of deepened understanding of and appreciation for our theological/doctrinal foundations. To the bishops I shall always be grateful.

The congregation and staff of Church Street Church merit special expressions of gratitude. They supported my devotion of time to study and writing, and they heard first most of the sermons in this volume. Their healthy pride in our Wesleyan heritage, their openness to theological exploration, their commitment to sound doctrine, and their tradition of strong worship provide an invigorating climate for preaching. It is an honor to be part of a faith community that considers theology the essence of its identity rather than an option for a study or sermon series.

Contents

Introduction: Doctrinal Preaching...................................... 11

Part One: Sermons on Our Theological Task

The Church's Search for Identity.. 15
  Understanding The Church As a Theological Community
  Matt. 5:13-16; I Peter 2:1-10
Nourished by Our Roots..22
  Value of Remembering Our Doctrinal Heritage
  Deut. 6:1-5; II Tim. 1:3-14
Balancing Beliefs and Behavior.. 29
  Sound Doctrine and Holy Living
  Matt. 7:21-28; James 1:14-26
The Tough Mind and the Tender Heart............................36
  Knowledge and Vital Piety
  Matt. 10:16-20; John 8:31-33
Tools for the Task.. 43
  Scripture, Tradition, Reason, Experience
  Acts 17:16-34

Part Two: Sermons on Our Doctrinal Beliefs

Transforming Grace.. 52
  Prevenient, Justifying, and Sanctifying Grace
  Eph. 2:1-10
Going on to Perfection...57
  Sanctification, Perfection
  Matt. 5:43-48; Phil. 3:12-21

Being Saved Isn't Enough......................................64
Personal Salvation and Social Witness
Luke 10:25-37

On Being Two-Thirds Wesleyan...........................70
Stewardship
Luke 16:1-13

◆ ◆ ◆

The God Beyond Our Knowing.............................76
The Unfinished Task of Theology
Exod. 3:1-15; 33:12-23

United by a Shared Faith.....................................82
Catholic Spirit
John 17:11b-21

Notes...88
Resources for Further Study................................91

Introduction:
Doctrinal Preaching

United Methodism in recent history has not been noted for doctrinal preaching. Life-situation or pastoral preaching has received major attention from the pulpits, especially in the wake of the formidable influence of Harry Emerson Fosdick and the advent of popular psychology. "Relevant" preaching has become synonymous with offering psychological solutions to personal problems, such as feelings of inferiority, disappointment, negative thinking, failure, bad tempers, and so forth. Topics for sermons arise out of the felt needs or wishes of the people.

In the 1960s, a wave of social activism broke upon some quarters of the church and swept some preachers into the current of controversial sociopolitical issues. Preachers scanned the newspapers for sermon topics and looked to sociology, economics, and political science for answers to perplexing social problems.

Much preaching, however, cannot be categorized as either life-situation or social-issue preaching. It falls into the realm of institutional promotion—encouraging attendance, tithing, teaching in church school, and serving the institution. The calendar for special days and the institutional needs of the local church have become primary sources of sermon topics.

Lectionary preaching appears to be on the increase throughout the denomination. If the lectionary puts preachers in touch with the biblical and theological foundations of the community of faith, then the result may be the recovery of the church's identity. If, however, the lectionary is used as a biblical underpinning for sociological and psychological analyses and institutional promotion, then it will only intensify the church's identity confusion.

Life situations, social issues, institutional concerns, and promotion are legitimate themes for sermons. The problem arises when they are only superficially related to the church's doctrinal/theological foundation. All preaching is basically theological; that is, its motive and focus emerge from a grappling with the reality and purposes of God. Preaching that lacks doctrinal/theological integrity becomes something other than preaching—a lecture in psychology, sociology, or politics, or a cheerleading session for institutional advancement.

United Methodists have tended to accept the popular myth that our church has minimal interest in doctrine. Structure and organization plus theological diversity have been considered defining characteristics. However, United Methodism's emphasis on doctrinal and theological diversity is not synonymous with indifferentism. Sound doctrine and theological exploration in the light of emerging personal and social issues are hallmarks of our Wesleyan heritage. Wesley's written sermons are predominantly doctrinal sermons that relate beliefs to personal life and social concerns.

United Methodist lay persons are vitally interested in basic Christian beliefs. Preaching that seeks to clarify and apply basic beliefs will be heard with appreciation. Wesley considered sermons to be effective tools for teaching and evangelization. Recovery of the teaching role of preaching is needed at this juncture of the church's history.

Preaching on United Methodist beliefs and doctrine can be exciting and invigorating for the preacher and the congregation. The following are offered as suggestions to preachers.

First, study the doctrinal/theological statement approved by The General Conference. It contains an excellent summary of our doctrinal heritage, the beliefs we share in common with other communions, the distinctive emphases of United Methodism, and our theological method.

Second, read the sermons by John Wesley. The volumes edited by Albert Outler, which began publication in 1984, contain Wesley's sermons along with insightful introductions and notes by Dr. Outler. The sermons are rich sources of insight, even though the structure and style may be more didactic than is appropriate in the contemporary pulpit. Remember that Wesley's written sermons were for the purpose of education and that, according to Outler, they do not reflect Wesley's oral style of communication.

Third, a series of sermons on United Methodist beliefs has more depth and far-reaching results if preached in conjunction with a discussion or study of the doctrinal/theological statement. During the weeks that I preached the sermons in this volume, I also led a thirteen-session discussion of *Doctrinal Standards and Our Theological Task*. The classroom provided opportunity for feedback on the sermons, and the sermons were supplemented by the classroom discussion.

Fourth, deciding which beliefs or emphases to include in the series may be the most difficult aspect of the preparation. I chose to include the basic emphases of the doctrinal/theological statement. Because *Doctrinal Standards and Our Theological Task* distinguishes between doctrine and theological exploration, it seemed appropriate to divide the sermons into these two categories. It should be understood that within the two divisions of this book, all sermons contain both doctrine and theological reflection. Preaching about belief always should contain both content and process. Many options for sermons in such a series exist. A whole series, for example, could be developed around Wesley's understanding of grace; or a series focusing on the ethical principles reflected in the General Rules would be beneficial.

A fifth suggestion relates to the structure of the sermon and the method of preparation. The temptation may be to take Wesley's points and build a new sermon around them. Wesley's sermon "The Use of Money" became the framework for the sermon that I entitled "On Being Two-Thirds Wesleyan." However, that sermon is the exception in this volume. The more prevalent approach consisted of the following steps: 1) identifying the basic belief, 2) studying biblical passages in which the belief is grounded, 3) reviewing the doctrinal/theological statement on the particular belief, 4) reading Wesley's sermon(s) on the subject, 5) formulating a propositional summary of the sermon's focus and content, 6) gathering other relevant material, such as illustrations and other quotations, 7) outlining the sermon and writing a manuscript, 8) delivering the sermon, and 9) revising in light of feedback and responses.

Two comments from parishioners who heard these sermons confirmed my decision to preach them. One said, "The sermons on United Methodist beliefs are helping us to get back to the basics. It is easy for us to get caught up in peripheral matters and lose touch with the bedrock of faith. Your sermons on basic beliefs help us to keep our feet on solid ground." Another comment came from a relatively new United Methodist. She remarked, "I joined the United Methodist Church partly because of its openness to diversity and its willingness to confront social issues. I assumed, though, that we really didn't have strong doctrines. The sermons on United Methodist beliefs helped me to see that we can be diverse and involved as well as take theology seriously."

It is because we take doctrine and theology seriously that we are diverse and involved. No other foundation is sufficient to sustain creative diversity and redemptive involvement.

Part One:
Sermons on Our Theological Task

Like living stones, let yourselves be built into a spiritual house, to be a holy priesthood, to offer spiritual sacrifices acceptable to God through Jesus Christ.

(*I Peter 2:5, NRSV*)

Matthew 5:13-16; I Peter 2:1-10

The Church's Search for Identity

The nineteenth-century Hindu philosopher Ramakrishna told a fable about a tiger cub who was separated from his mother and fellow tigers. He was adopted by goats who raised him as if he were a goat. So, instead of roaring with a voice that shook the forest, the tiger bleated softly in sounds heard only by his adopted family. Instead of eating red meat, the tiger grazed on the soft grass and ate bark from tender saplings, which caused him to lack the robust strength characteristic of well-fed tigers. Instead of roaming the lofty peaks and leaping the treacherous mountain crevices, the tiger who thought he was a goat roamed the paths of the lowlands. He didn't know who he was. His only image of himself was taken from the world around him, a world of goats rather than of tigers. He was less than a tiger because he had no understanding of what it meant to be a tiger. He had been cut off from his true identity.

The church suffers from a similar malady. We have been orphaned by our broken connection with our biblical and theological parentage. Our failure to stay in daily contact with the images of the church as found in the Bible and in historical theology has left us with the inadequate images of the world around us as our models of being and doing. The business world, civic clubs, and social and political organizations have become our patterns. Consequently, the church is treated as an institution among institutions—an organization among many

15

organizations to which we belong, in which we find fellowship, and in which we engage in endless activities.

The result is that we wander around on the smooth, well-worn lowland paths, grazing on tasty but unnourishing pious junk food. No one trembles at our blah messages or pays much attention to our bleating pronouncements. We hear the echo of a distant roar which temporarily strikes a responsive curiosity. We have a vague hunger that is not satisfied by palatable pious platitudes. Occasionally we glimpse a lofty height, or a Christlike image falls momentarily across our path, giving us a nudge to be more than we are as a church. We go through the motions, but our hearts are elsewhere. We know deep down in our souls that there is more to this church thing than going to meetings and promoting an institution.

Confusion regarding the church's identity is no recent development. John Wesley wrote in 1785, "How much do we almost continually hear about the Church! . . . And yet how few understand what they talk of! How few know what the term means! A more ambiguous word than this, the 'church', is scarce to be found in the English language."[1] In 1789, at the age of eighty-five, Wesley wrote a sermon entitled "Causes of the Inefficacy of Christianity." He raised the concern that Christianity—and particularly the Methodists—has not been more effective in transforming the world. One reason he gave is that so few have an understanding of the basic doctrines and beliefs of the faith. Before the church can be effective, according to Wesley, it must know the doctrines, practice the disciplines, and give itself sacrificially in obedience to Jesus Christ. In other words, Christianity's effectiveness requires that we know our true identity and live out that identity in the world.[2]

Our basic identity is rooted in theology, not sociology. In other words, the search for our true identity must lead us in the direction of examining God's presence in the world and God's purposes for the church. Images for who we are as the church are to be found in the Bible's witness to the reality and activity of God and in the historic affirmations of the church's faith.

The prevailing and pervasive understanding of the church today, however, is rooted in sociology. Rather than such images as *people of God, Body of Christ, royal priesthood, holy nation,* or

> *"When the world furnishes our identity, the mission of the church is defined in terms of strengthening the institution. . . ."*

community of faith being the controlling metaphors for our life and work, these are the images that come to mind when we think church: buildings, budgets, conferences, meetings, boards, committees, agencies, and programs. Management by objectives, strategic planning, marketing techniques, organizational structures, institutional maintenance—these have become the *modus operandi* of the contemporary church. Prayer has been reduced to a functionary way to open meetings. Bible study often is nothing but an attempt to find biblical quotations to support our narcissistic and programmatic pursuits. Worship of the Holy One has degenerated into an ecclesiastical version of "The Lawrence Welk Hour," or "The Ed Sullivan Variety Show," or "Saturday Night Live," or "The Gong Show"— depending on your taste in entertainment and what attracts a crowd.

When the world furnishes our identity, the mission of the church is defined in terms of strengthening the institution rather than in transforming the world. Evangelism is equated with church membership rather than with enabling persons to know themselves and others as free and forgiven daughters and sons of God. Ministry becomes a profession—a career to be cultivated and promoted—rather than a calling to be fulfilled; and pastors function as institutional CEOs rather than as visionaries of a new heaven and a new earth and mediators of the grace of God. Church leaders look to the sociology of church growth for renewal more than they look to the theology of personal and social transformation.

While Christ dies on a cross—bloody and bruised—for a broken world, the church—his new body—is preoccupied with its size, its reproductive rate, and the attractiveness of its features. While Christ lives and serves among the poor, the addicted, the imprisoned, and the wounded and sick, the

17

church is at the beauty shop trying to become more appealing to the masses. It is at the public relations firm working on a new slogan or marketing technique by which it hopes to win more admirers and members, or it is in the corporate boardroom developing a strategy to stop the downward slide of its membership. But the church's survival is never dependent upon its membership rolls; it is dependent upon the faithfulness of its members to their God-given roles. It is not our identity as a social institution that the world needs. The world needs the fulfillment of our identity as a redemptive community of God's faithful people—a movement of God's spirit in the hurting places of the world God loves.

The New Testament contains a multitude of rich models or images that define who we are as a church. I mention two that focus the church as a mission and as a nurturing community— an understanding deeply rooted in our Wesleyan heritage.

Matthew's Gospel was written a generation after Jesus' death. Members of this new community of Christ, in which the Risen Christ was present and proclaimed, were in danger of losing their identity. The gospel writer sought to keep the life, teaching, death, and resurrection of Jesus Christ before the community. He knew that only in so doing would the community remember and fulfill its true identity. Among Matthew's images are these reminders from the Christ: "You are the light of the world," and "You are the salt of the earth" (Matt. 5:13, 14, NRSV).

"You are the light of the world; a city set on a hill cannot be hid" (Matt. 5:14, NRSV). The church is a beacon community. It is a community of people who live God's vision for the world. In our personal lives and our life together we are to model for the world God's presence and purposes.

I once served a church that was located in the flight pattern of the regional airport. The spire of the church was lighted at night. It could be seen by the pilots as they made their approaches for landing or as they took off. One Sunday morning a pilot attended worship in our little church. After the service he told the handful of worshipers, "For years I have been using the lights from this church to get my bearings in the night.

I'm sure glad you keep your light beaming." The church is to be a light by which people keep their bearings.

One day the king tiger approached the herd of goats that had adopted the tiger cub. The goats scattered, leaving the tiger alone with the king tiger. The king tiger confronted the tiger who thought he was a goat with his true identity, but the tiger didn't understand. So the king tiger took the tiger to a stream. There the tiger saw his likeness to the king tiger, but he still did not feel or act like a tiger. Then the king tiger gave him some red meat. At first it tasted bitter, but soon it satisfied his deep hunger. It was then that the tiger roared his first roar—a roar that shook the whole forest.

"We are to be the body of Christ in the world. . . ."

Christ, the sovereign of humanity, has come to show us our identity. In him we see that we are sons and daughters of the Redeeming, Liberating God. He feeds us the often bitter meat of divine truth, but our hungers are satisfied with no less. We are to be the body of Christ in the world, by which bruised and alienated people are led to the living water where they see themselves as made in the divine image. Through the church's proclamation of the vision of God's justice and shalom, the world's peoples are to taste the bread that satisfies the hungry heart. Our doctrines and affirmations and our creeds and theologies become the meat that nourishes the soul and challenges the mind.

Light exposes the evils, and it heals, nurtures, and beckons us toward new horizons. It pushes back the darkness of despair and opens the curtain of a new dawn. That's who we are. We are a sign of God's reign breaking out in the world. We are a community in which God's future invades the present.

"You are the salt of the earth" (Matt. 5:13, NRSV). Salt preserves and gives taste and zest. The church is a light, a mission, but it is also a preserving and nurturing community.

19

One means by which we serve as agents of God's redeeming, reconciling, and healing presence is by preserving the values, the truths, and the doctrines of our heritage. The great insights, stories, liturgies, and memories of our heritage are kept alive and active. We teach them, refine them, and incorporate them into our life together. In so doing, we are shaped by God's Eternal Word rather than by the shifting currents of societal preferences.

The church as the salt of the earth preserves the identity of its own fellowship through love. The church is to be both the community's conscience and a compassionate community. The church is a community of grace, not a cozy fellowship of nice people trying to be nicer. This community of grace, like salt or red meat, has a bitter edge to it. These people who make up the church have come together because Christ died for them. That is serious business. We are part of this community of the Crucified One not because of our merit, but simply because the Crucified and Risen One invites us to be his body. Therefore, barriers of race and class and sex have no place in the community. Everybody is somebody. Worth in this community is based upon to whom we belong, not upon anything else. Therefore, all are treated with respect and dignity—like kings and queens, like daughters and sons of God, like brothers and sisters of the Christ.

> *"A church rooted in theology is a beacon community in a world that has lost its way."*

A woman who struggled with the scars of sexual exploitation and abuse had this to say about a congregation that treated her with dignity and value: "Every time I enter the sanctuary I feel as though I am being hugged by God." That's who we are—a community in which people feel hugged by God.

A young man, twenty years of age, had been on drugs and alcohol for eight years. He was arrested several times. Family members were at their wits' end. He landed in jail. No one would bail him out. He realized that if he ever was going to be free from his enslavement he would have to find a new peer group. He went to the United Methodist Church where his grandparents were members. A college-age Sunday school class took him in. A Sunday-evening Bible study group welcomed him. Through the help of the pastor and some lay people, he was accepted into a halfway house. When he later was received into church membership by profession of faith, he said to the congregation, "Thank you for helping me when I couldn't help myself." He is now enrolled in a church-related college. His life is being transformed by a nurturing community of grace called the church. That kind of love is the salt of the earth.

The world desperately needs a church that knows who it is. A church whose identity is rooted in sociology is of marginal relevance. A church that is rooted in theology—that knows what it believes and practices what it believes—is a beacon community in a world that has lost its way; and it has a roar before which the whole forest trembles. Let us recover that identity by rediscovering our doctrinal/theological foundation and building upon it.

I close with these words from John Wesley:

> In the meantime let all those who are real members of the church see that they walk holy and unblamable in all things. Ye are the light of the world!' . . . Ye are 'a city set upon a hill, and cannot be hid. O let your light shine before men [others]!' Show them your faith by your works. Let them see by the whole tenor of your conversation that your hope is all laid up above! Let all your words and actions evidence the spirit whereby you are animated! Above all things, let your love abound. Let it extend to every child of man [humanity]; let it overflow to every child of God. By this let all men [people] know whose disciples ye are, because you love one another.[3]

> *Hold to the standard of sound teaching that you
> have heard from me, in the faith and love that are
> in Christ Jesus. Guard the good treasure entrusted to
> you, with the help of the Holy Spirit living in us.*
>
> (II Timothy 1: 13-14 , NRSV)

Deuteronomy 6:1-5; II Timothy 1:3-14

Nourished by Our Roots

A woman in the early stages of Alzheimer's disease expressed her fear of being robbed of her memories. "I won't remember who I am," she said, holding back the tears. "I'll forget the family I belong to. I won't have any roots. Without them, I would rather be dead."

Our roots—our memories—mold and shape and define us. Without roots, we lose our identity. We have no anchor to hold us when the storms rage and the winds blow. We have no foundation to support us. We feel disconnected and isolated. Cut off from our roots, we wither and die.

The Bible expresses the importance of remembering our roots. Deuteronomy became an important book after the fall of Israel. It was rediscovered in the southern kingdom of Judah during the reign of Josiah, around 621 B.C. Judah faced possible destruction. How could the people avoid the fate of their northern kinfolk, Israel? Deuteronomy's prescription for survival was that the nation remember its roots. By recalling God's mighty acts, by remembering the Law, and by retelling the story, they could avoid the mistake of their neighbors who had forgotten the Lord their God.

On the night before his death, when all that he represented was threatened, Jesus took a loaf and a cup. He said to his disciples, "Do this in remembrance of me" (Luke 22:19, NRSV). We continue to be nourished by that act of remembrance. While hanging on the cross against a dark sky, Jesus expressed his feelings in a psalm from his heritage: "My God, my God, why have you forsaken me?" (Matt. 27:46; Psalm 22:1, NRSV).

John Wesley knew the writings of the Bible and the early church leaders as well as anyone in eighteenth-century England. He did not see himself as the founder of a new church or the author of new doctrines. Rather, he considered his role to be a recoverer of the ancient traditions and practices of the faith.

In a letter to Wesley, William Dodd wrote that he had given up all historical authority. Wesley responded with this sharply worded reply: "You say, 'You set aside all authority, ancient and modern.' Sir, who told you so? I never did; it never entered my thoughts. Who it was gave you that rule I know not; but my father gave it [to] me thirty years ago (I mean concerning reverence to the ancient church and our own), and I have endeavored to walk by it to this day."[1]

> *"Cut off from our doctrinal roots, we fall prey to the promises of pop religion. . . ."*

We in the contemporary church may be closer to Dodd's attitude than to Wesley's. The church suffers from a life-threatening case of amnesia. Severed from our roots, we search for identity along the unpromising path of institutional success. Cut off from our doctrinal roots, we are easy prey for the promises of pop religion and the cult of narcissistic self-gratification. The judgment of Deuteronomy 32:18 well could be our fate: "You were unmindful of the Rock that bore you; you forgot the God who gave you birth" (NRSV).

The creeds and affirmations of our heritage, the Articles of Religion and Confessions of Faith, the writings of our forebears, the hymns and liturgies of our ancestors—these are roots that nourish, mold, and shape the church. They are precious gifts from our fathers and mothers in the faith. They are avenues of God's presence and purposes. These doctrinal and theological roots provide us with three indispensable resources.

First, our roots provide a foundation on which to stand and upon which to build. The historic creeds, ancient affirmations of faith, collections of prayers and hymns, and writings of reformers and preachers are deposits of faith upon which we draw when life seems bankrupt and everything that once was nailed down begins to come loose.

Some friends of mine lost their twenty-two-year-old son in a tragic automobile accident. When we gathered in the sanctuary for the funeral service, we sang some of the great hymns of the church. We affirmed our faith by saying the Apostles' Creed. The choir offered a choral arrangement of Psalm 23. We prayed prayers from our liturgy. Some weeks following the service, the grieving mother said something like this: "I was too hurt to sing the hymns and I couldn't really say the creed with confidence. But when I couldn't sing or affirm my faith, the church did it for me. When it seemed that life had fallen apart, the church reminded me that the foundation stands firm."

The historic creeds, the liturgies, the affirmations, and the hymns that often have been tried in the fires of persecution, forged on the anvil of controversy, and tested by the challenge of the ages provide a place to stand when life is shattered and faith is threatened. They provide a mooring for a church called to navigate the turbulent waters of an increasingly secularized and dangerous age. In a time of danger and threat, the Deuteronomist called upon the people to write the commandments upon their hearts, to teach the commandments to their children, and to bind the commandments as a sign upon their hands—so "they shall be as frontlets between your eyes" (Deut. 6:6-8, RSV). Likewise, Timothy, who was young and inexperienced in the faith, was advised by the wise and more experienced apostle Paul, "Hold to the standard of sound teaching that you have heard. . . . Guard the good treasure entrusted to you" (II Tim. 1:13-14, NRSV). Stay connected to your roots; stand on the foundation laid by God's action in the past.

Second, our roots in the historic creeds and affirmations help us to establish boundaries and parameters in our search for authentic and valid faith. The notion that there are no boundaries and parameters has become popular in recent years

24

in The United Methodist Church. A misreading of the emphasis on pluralism and diversity and a misuse of our doctrinal guidelines—Scripture, tradition, reason, and experience—led some United Methodists to assume that historic doctrines are unimportant.

> *"The woods are full of popular proclaimers of appealing heresies."*

A middle-aged man shared with me a conversation that he had with a United Methodist pastor. The conversation took place at a time when he was going through some serious intellectual struggles. He had put his religious beliefs in a forgotten mental hideaway; yet, he had a longing for transcendence and meaning which he hoped he could find by returning to the church of his childhood. He went to the pastor and inquired what United Methodists believe. The pastor responded by saying that United Methodists don't really have a set of doctrines because we believe that people should think and let think. The preacher proceeded to explain that persons could come to their own beliefs through Scripture, tradition, reason, and experience. The man replied, "But I have to have someplace to begin—some framework within which Scripture, tradition, reason, and experience become relevant."

Heresy, or false teaching, has persistently threatened the church. Today is no exception. The woods are full of popular proclaimers of appealing heresies. We are most susceptible to follow them when our faith is rooted in shallow soil rather than in the fertile and deep soil of history.

In an interview with Religious News Service in 1986, Will Campbell bemoaned the departure of Southern Baptists from their roots in the tenets of the Reformation. He suggested that much of contemporary heresy would be avoided if Southern Baptists would read history. Then, in his characteristic fashion, Campbell chided his colleagues—not to mention many of us—

with the charge that they "spend more time blow drying their hair than wrestling with their history."[2] Well, his charge is not true of this preacher, but that says more about the amount of my hair than the extent of my history reading.

Campbell is right: we have departed from our doctrinal and theological roots. Let us remember that the Deuteronomist called upon the former slaves to remember their faith heritage, so that when they reached the Promised Land they would not fall victim to the heresy that it was by their might and their power that they had become free and prosperous. Staying connected to our roots enables us to stand when all about us is shifting and when circumstances threaten to undo our faith. A church nourished by its doctrinal and theological roots provides parameters and markers for our continuing faith pilgrimage.

> *"We are defined and identified by . . . the community in which we claim identity."*

Third, our doctrinal roots tie us to the community of God's people. We are defined and identified by the company we keep—the community in which we claim identity. We parents know that. We are very concerned when our children become part of "communities" whose values and behaviors are contrary to those we wish for them. We know that people are molded and shaped by their communities.

I know a woman who was adopted as an infant. Since she didn't know her birth parents, she felt that a significant part of her identity was missing. As an adult she learned the identity of her biological parents. After months of anxious waiting, she made arrangements to meet them. Not all such meetings turn out well, but this one did. She shared with me the joy of learning that her parents really loved her but gave her up because of their inability to provide for her. They looked through old albums and scrapbooks together. She heard the stories of her family, and they became her stories. She said to me, "I learned that I was a part of a larger family that loved me too."

In Alex Haley's *Roots*, Kunta Kinte drove his master to a plantation ball. As Kunta Kinte relaxed in the carriage to wait for his master's return, he heard in the distance some sounds other than the white people's music. It was a different sound. His feet took him in the direction of the luring notes coming from the slaves' cabins. As he got closer, Kunta Kinte recognized the music to be that of his native African tribe. Upon entering the cabin, he found fellow slaves who had been taken from the same part of Africa as he. They conversed in their native tongues. They sang their native songs. They remembered their common heritage. Early the next morning, after he had returned to his quarters, Kunta Kinte lay on the dirt floor. Tears flowed from his eyes. They were tears of sadness for having almost forgotten who he was, and they were tears of joy for having remembered the community to which he belonged.

When we stand in a service of worship and share in the affirmation of the Apostles' Creed, we are claiming our identity in the community of St. Augustine of Hippo, St. Francis of Assisi, St. Teresa of Avila, Martin Luther, John Wesley, and a host of heroes of the faith. When we pray the Lord's Prayer, we are joining our brothers and sisters in the faith—from the apostles Peter and John to the reformers Calvin and Zwingli, from the early martyrs Polycarp and Irenaeus to the modern faith heroes Bonhoeffer and Martin Luther King, Jr. When we sing or read the psalms, we are joining the great cloud of witnesses that includes David, Isaiah, Jeremiah, Ezekiel, Hosea, and Amos. When we share psalms that Jesus learned at Mary's knee and sang in Nazareth's synagogue, we are making them our songs, too. When we read the letters of Paul, we are acknowledging that they are our letters. When we join in singing "O for a Thousand Tongues to Sing," we are claiming our place in the company of John and Charles Wesley, Francis Asbury, Philip William Otterbein, Jacob Albright, Barbara Heck, and the countless persons who have sat in the pew where you sit today.

Remember the rock from which you were hewn. We are part of the great company of God's people who through the ages have shared common stories, common creeds, and common liturgies. These are our roots. From these roots we receive the nourishment to grow toward the sunlight of new horizons of God's eternal purposes. These roots provide a place to stand. These roots define who we are. These roots shape our future. These roots enable us to know the God who is the Alpha and Omega, the beginning and the end.

> *Not everyone who says to me, "Lord, Lord," will enter the kingdom of heaven, but only the one who does the will of my Father in heaven.*
>
> (*Matthew 7:21, NRSV*)

Matthew 7:21-28; James 1:14-26

Balancing Beliefs and Behavior

While in college I worked during the summers on a construction crew. Two men with whom I worked, Ned and Joe, were fascinating characters. Ned's avocation was reading the Bible and studying religion. He knew the Bible from cover to cover and would have defeated all takers in Bible Trivial Pursuit. He knew the words of the Bible as well as anyone I have known. His life-style, on the other hand, left much to be desired. He was racially bigoted, insensitive, and sometimes dishonest.

The other character, Joe, never quoted the Bible. When Ned tried to engage Joe in a religious argument, Joe would respond, "I don't know what you are talking about. I don't know much about the Bible and those doctrines. The only important thing to me is how you live." Ned would counter, "But you must believe . . . ," and he would proceed to quote verses, usually taken out of context.

These two men dramatize a long-existing tension in theology—the tension between beliefs and behavior. Where do we put the emphasis? On behavior—living honorably, lovingly, and faithfully? Or is the emphasis to be placed on orthodox beliefs—having a clear understanding of what one believes?

How do we maintain the proper balance between beliefs and behavior, doctrine and discipline, faith and works? That has been a long-standing issue in the church. It appears that the

> *"Belief and behavior . . . cannot be separated without subverting both."*

Christian community generally has opted for an emphasis on one at the expense of the other.

John Wesley struggled with this tension all of his life. Spiritual heirs of Wesley continue to strive for balance between maintaining sound doctrine and practicing disciplined, holy living. John Wesley knew the doctrines of the church as well as anyone who lived in the eighteenth century. Scripture was so familiar to him that quoting verses was second nature to him. But Wesley also pursued holy living as arduously as anyone in history. In fact, he and his cohorts were first called *Methodists* as a result of their methodical approach to both sound doctrine and disciplined, holy living.

A favorite maxim of Wesley's that came from the early church is this: "The soul and the body make a man [person]; the spirit and discipline make a Christian."[1] Wesley interpreted the maxim to mean that we need both sound doctrine and Christian discipline. He contended that the weakness of the church of his day resulted from two failures: a lack of understanding of the basic beliefs, such as justification, God's providence, the meaning of Christ, and new birth; and/or a failure to practice discipline. Balance between belief and behavior is therefore our tradition—a tradition that desperately needs to be recovered in this age of fuzzy or rigidly held theology and anything-goes or narrowly moralistic behavior.

First, let us be clear that belief and behavior—sound doctrine and disciplined lives—cannot be separated without subverting both. Beliefs without behavior that emanates from those beliefs degenerate into irrelevancy. The result is a pigeonholed religion, one conveniently compartmentalized from the real world of decisions and relationships. Without an emphasis on behavior and practice, religious beliefs become merely speculative conjecture. Belief in God becomes as unimportant as belief in life on other planets. There may be planets out there that sustain life, but we have no relationship with them, and they certainly do not influence our behavior or decisions. The result is what may be referred to as *practical atheism*, which is living as if there were no God.

> *"Beliefs . . . that do not shape our lives, relationships, and actions are no more than religious trinkets. . . ."*

When the "death of God" controversy made the headlines in the 1960s, a man in our neighborhood became angry and belligerent when Thomas Altizer, one of the exponents of the concept, was allowed to teach at Emory University. Now, this man never attended church. He was proud of his hatred for everyone who was different from him, and he self-righteously contended that poor people were just lazy. He had accumulated his wealth through shady business deals, and he was generally meanspirited.

One day he stopped me as I entered the subdivision where he and I lived. He rolled down the window in his Cadillac and said angrily, "You Methodists aren't worth a damn. If you were, you'd get rid of that atheist at Emory!"

"Suppose Dr. Altizer is right and God is dead. What difference will that make in your life today?" I responded.

Staring angrily at me, he said, "None! But any fool knows that there is something up there who created this world." With that, he pushed the electronic button that rolled up his car window and he sped away. His belief in God made no difference in the shape and practice of his life.

Beliefs—however commendable and orthodox—that do not shape our lives, relationships, and actions are no more than religious trinkets locked away in a crowded closet. Jesus warned of the dangers of reducing religion to pious platitudes such as "Lord, Lord" and of failing to do the will of God. He said at the conclusion of the Sermon on the Mount, "And everyone who hears these words of mine and does not act on them will be like a foolish man who built his house on the sand" (Matt. 7:26, NRSV).

On the other hand, those who hear and do, those who believe and practice, build a house on a firm foundation. The Epistle of James may have been written in response to a misinterpretation of Paul's emphasis on belief in the efficacy of God's grace. Apparently, some persons had assumed that belief in justification by grace and grace alone meant that behavior did not matter. James warned, however, that failure to put faith into action results in the death of faith. "Faith without works is dead" (James 2:20, KJV). Beliefs without behavior, faith without works, and doctrine without discipline result in fragmentation of life and the loss of faith. But behavior without noble beliefs, discipline without sound doctrine, and works without liberating faith lead to unbearable tension, judgmental self-righteousness, and superficial legalism.

Some of us bear the scars of a religion that emphasizes being good in order to avoid God's punishment. An incident from my childhood left an indelible mark on me. Our family lived on several farms as sharecroppers during my early childhood. One day as my older brother and sister and I played on the lawn outside the big white house of the landowner, the landowner staggered from around the corner of the house. He was drunk. Earlier that day he had ordered me to get off of one of the farm buildings. As he came toward me he said, "I'm going to teach you to respect me and my property. I'm going to drown you in the rain barrel." He picked me up by the heels and carried me to the rain barrel at the corner of the house. He dangled me over that pit of destruction until his wife grabbed him from behind and forced him to leave me alone. But from thenceforth he boasted of how he made me "shape up." Outwardly, I treated him with respect. It was always, "Yes, sir," or "No, sir," or "Thank you, sir." But inside I had no respect for him at all.

I had some of the same fears in church. Week after week I heard the preacher warn in a strident voice of anger that we were going to hell if we did not repent of our wrongdoing and behave as God would have us to behave. That was deeply ingrained in my psyche, and for years I lived in mortal fear of God. My behavior was motivated not by genuine belief in a loving and liberating God but by terror of a God whom I did not trust or love. Learning to trust and love God has been a lifelong struggle, and being rid of a compulsive need to earn love by behaving properly continues to be the work of divine grace in my life.

Like a cut flower, behavior that is based on the desire to please, on efforts to gain worth, or on fear simply withers and dies. This kind of behavior is like plastic lilies; they may appear beautiful, but they have no life. We become "whitewashed tombs" (Matt. 23:27, NRSV), outwardly clean but inwardly dead, lifeless. In the Bible, proper behavior is a response to a belief or faith in a God who is acting on our behalf. Note how beliefs and behavior, doctrine and discipline, and faith and works are connected in the Bible. God's requirements, God's commands, are preceded by God's action.

The Shema is the summary of the Old Testament image of belief and behavior. "Hear, O Israel: The Lord our God is one Lord" (Deut. 6:4, RSV). That is the belief. Then follows the appropriate response: "You shall love the Lord your God with all your heart, and with all your soul, and with all your might" (Deut. 6:5, RSV). That is behavior, response!

The Ten Commandments are prefaced with these words: "I am the Lord your God, who brought you out of the land of Egypt, out of the house of slavery" (Exod. 20:2, NRSV). That is faith, belief, doctrine. The commandments represent the appropriate behavior in response to God's mighty act of deliverance from slavery.

In Mark's Gospel, Jesus walked along the lakeside announcing, "The time is fulfilled, and the kingdom of God has come near" (Mark 1:15, NRSV). That's affirmation! That's belief! That's doctrine! God is bringing a new world! Now comes the appropriate response: "Repent, and believe in the good news" (Mark 1:15, NRSV). All of Jesus' demands—from "Come follow me" to "Take up your cross"; from "Go sell all you have and give to the poor" to "Turn the other cheek and go the second mile"—are rooted in the affirmation of the dawning of God's kingdom as a gift from God.

In Galatians Paul affirms, "For freedom Christ has set us free" (Gal. 5:1, NRSV). That's belief! That's sound doctrine! Christ has set us free! Then comes the expected behavioral response: "Stand firm, therefore, and do not submit again to a yoke of slavery. . . . For you were called to freedom, brothers and sisters" (Gal. 5:1, 13, NRSV). Belief! Affirmation! Doctrine! "Only do not use your freedom as an opportunity for self-indulgence, but through love become slaves to one another" (Gal. 5:13, NRSV). That is disciplined, holy living in response to sound doctrine.

"Beliefs and behavior are held together by gratitude. . . ."

Hear Paul again: "In Christ God was reconciling the world to himself, not counting their trespasses against them" (II Cor. 5:19, NRSV). That is sound doctrine! God has acted decisively in Jesus Christ to reconcile us to God, to our true selves, and to others! What is the behavior to be balanced with this good news? "And entrusting the message of reconciliation to us. So we are ambassadors for Christ, since God is making his appeal through us" (II Cor. 5:19-20, NRSV).

Beliefs and behavior are held together, then, by gratitude—gratitude for God's belief in us and God's gracious behavior toward us and the world. Gratitude transforms obedience from dreaded duty to a joyful expression of love. We simply enjoy doing what we do out of gratitude and love.

A father was trying to persuade his son and daughter to clean the house before their mother returned home from a business trip. The children grumbled and procrastinated. Finally, the father said, "You know, Mom has been very good to us. She works hard and long and she loves us very much. No doubt she will come in the door with a hug and gift for us. Why don't we give her something in return. Let's give her a clean house." The boy and girl busily cleaned the house, whistling and singing and laughing. A clean house became a grateful response to a loving parent. That is behavior linked to belief. That is works balanced by faith.

34

Much has been made by United Methodists about John Wesley's experience at Aldersgate—more than Wesley himself made of it. It was an important milestone in his spiritual and psychological pilgrimage. The importance of Wesley's "heart-warming experience" was that it gave balance to practice and belief in his life. Prior to Aldersgate, Wesley's efforts had been directed toward holy living as a means of justification. In other words, he sought to behave properly in order to be loved by God. When he personally accepted the belief that Christ had died for him, that God loved him unconditionally, he then sought holiness of heart and life in response to having been justified. Wesley spent the rest of his life proclaiming sound doctrine and calling for disciplined living.

God has claimed us as God's own children. That is belief. We seek to live holy, disciplined lives. That is appropriate response. Belief and behavior! Doctrine and discipline! Faith and works! God's gracious action on behalf of humankind and humankind's grateful obedience in response—that is the gospel!

> *If you continue in my word, you are truly my*
> *disciples; and you will know the truth, and the*
> *truth will make you free.*
>
> (*John 8:31-32, NRSV*)

Matthew 10:16-20; John 8:31-33

The Tough Mind
and the Tender Heart

The eighteenth century was a remarkable era. Among its sons and daughters were some of history's greatest minds and noblest spirits. Historians have characterized the eighteenth century as the Age of Reason. During this time there were many towering intellects who fueled what twentieth century minds have called "the knowledge explosion." Scientists such as Isaac Newton and Joseph Priestley added to the revolutionary developments of Copernicus and Galileo and Kepler. Philosophers such as Jean-Jacques Rousseau, Voltaire, David Hume, and Adam Smith pushed the mind in bold directions.

Propelled by fresh ideas of freedom and human dignity, great minds such as Thomas Jefferson, Benjamin Franklin, and Thomas Paine put their reason to work in the building of a nation. Poets and novelists extolled the virtues of human capacity. Deism and rationalism were dominant *isms*. The tough mind was respected and revered.

However, another phenomenon gained prominence during the eighteenth century: religious fervor. It also was a century of revivalism and piety. The Wesley brothers, John and Charles, spread their message of heartwarming religion nurtured by disciplined habits and expressed in holy living. On the American frontier, the Great Awakening took place under the leadership of George Whitefield, who supposedly could say

36

Mesopotamia and make people cry. The woods of the new land and the villages of the old world were alive with the prayers and hymns of people who felt their hearts strangely warmed with a message of salvation from sin. It was what some historians have called the Age of Faith.

> *"This false dichotomy between thinkers and feelers . . . pulls the church apart."*

This dichotomy presented a problem. People seemed to choose between faith and reason, the head and the heart, the mind and the emotions. In a sermon preached at Wesley Theological Seminary in 1980, Dr. Clarence Goen referred to the period as the "Century of the Great Divorce." Reason and revelation were divorced, knowledge and piety were estranged, reason and faith were disunited, and the tough mind and the tender heart were separated. Like offspring of a divorce, the people began to choose between parents—Father Faith or Mother Mind. We are the offspring of that divorce. This false dichotomy between thinkers and feelers—between faith as reasoned beliefs and faith as evangelical experience, between knowledge and piety—pulls the church apart and leaves faith pilgrims confused about which to follow: the head or the heart.

On one hand, there are those who confine religion to pious feelings, simple trust, and holy habits. Education or knowledge is considered to be a seducer that distracts us from authentic piety. When my home church said good-bye to a son in the faith who was going off to seminary, a genuinely pious member had this advice: "Don't let those educated professors destroy your faith." Likewise, one devoted member of my own family thought I was wasting my time going to school in order to be a preacher. "All you need to know is that Jesus is your Savior, and you don't have to be educated to know that. God will give you all you have to know," she said. Piety, in other words, has little to do with knowledge. The warm heart can get along better without a head full of knowledge.

37

On the other hand, others would counter that religion is basically intellectual. These individuals treat personal piety with scorn—with an air of intellectual snobbery and suspicion. "Get your head straight, your beliefs in order, and your knowledge digested; then you will be OK," they might say. Hard calculations and meticulously consistent doctrines take precedence over heartwarming feelings of divine presence.

The result of this dichotomy is a schizophrenic church, a fragmented faith, and a discipleship with either all heart and no head or all head and no heart. Like the characters in *The Wizard of Oz*, we are either Tin Man disciples—with brains but no hearts—or Scarecrow disciples—with hearts but no brains— who are in search of the Wizard, or God, or meaning, or purpose, or whatever it is we call ultimate.

Yet, the people called Methodists achieved a balance between piety and knowledge in the Age of the Great Divorce. We are the offspring of those ancestors. The Wesleyan balance is expressed most clearly in a hymn written by Charles Wesley that contains this admonition of the people called Methodists: "Let us unite the pair so long disjoined, knowledge and vital piety."[1]

John Wesley was asked this question by co-workers: "Why is it that the people under our care are no better?" He replied, "Because we are not more knowing and more holy." The studious and pious Wesley then admonished the preachers to read and study: "Steadily spend all the morning in this employ, or, at least, five hours in four-and-twenty."[2] We need to be reminded that Wesley and his cohorts were first called Methodists not because of their methodical organization but because of their disciplined method of achieving knowledge and piety. Wesley not only established class meetings for the purpose of pursuing vital piety, but he also founded Kingswood School for the education of the mind. Likewise, when the Methodist Episcopal Church was organized in America at the Christmas Conference of 1784, the new church not only adopted the Articles of Religion and the Orders of Worship, but its members also voted to found a college—Cokesbury College.

The wedding of the mind and the heart—of knowledge and piety—is rooted in the New Testament. After all, our Lord

"Effectiveness requires a tough mind and a tender heart."

summarized discipleship as loving God with all of one's heart, strength, and mind. When he summoned the apostles and sent them into a hostile, demon-filled, alien world, Jesus gave them this charge: "I am sending you out like sheep into the midst of wolves; so be wise as serpents and innocent as doves" (Matt. 10:16, NRSV). In other words, effectiveness requires a tough mind and a tender heart; discipleship requires both vital piety and knowledge.

Knowledge without piety is less than authentic personhood and genuine discipleship. Intelligence and education in and of themselves are not virtues. A tough mind without a heart made sensitive and humble by grace and love can be demonic. Knowledge apart from values rooted in human dignity and compassion for all creation may yet destroy us. In a daring sermon preached at Oxford University, John Wesley said, "Without love all learning is but splendid ignorance, pompous folly."[3]

Piety without knowledge, however, becomes sentimentalized emotionalism. Religion without intellect becomes the enemy of science by wasting its energies on such marginal issues as evolution verses creationism and the inerrancy of scripture. Piety without knowledge resisted the use of anesthesia, persecuted Galileo and Copernicus, and argued for the flatness of the earth. In this century it led nine hundred people to drink strychnine in Jonestown. Today it is seeking to purge some theological seminaries of their finest scholarship, and in some parts of the world it is persecuting and terrorizing populations in the name of God or Allah or Jesus.

Piety needs knowledge and knowledge needs piety. Wesley said to those who despise or depreciate reason: "You must not imagine you are doing God a service; least of all are you promoting the cause of God when you are endeavouring to exclude reason out of religion. . . . You see it directs us in every point both of faith and practice: it guides us with regard to every branch both of inward and outward holiness."[4] To those who overvalue reason, however, Wesley warned:

> Let reason do all that reason can: employ it as far as it will go. But, at the same time acknowledge it is utterly incapable of giving either faith, or hope, or love; and consequently of producing either real virtue or substantial happiness. Expect those from a higher source. . . . Seek and receive them not as your own acquisition, but as the gift of God. . . . So shall you be living witnesses that wisdom, holiness, and happiness are one, are inseparably united. . . . [5]

"Jesus Christ is the incarnation of the mind and heart of God."

Piety and knowledge are united in Christ Jesus. To put it another way, piety and knowledge remain integrally related when they emerge from faith in and commitment to God revealed in Jesus Christ. Hear these words from John's Gospel: "If you continue in my word, you are truly my disciples; and you will know the truth, and the truth will make you free" (John 8:31-32, NRSV). There it is! Truth—liberating truth—and discipleship—or piety—grow out of a relationship with Jesus Christ.

Jesus Christ is the incarnation of the mind and heart of God. Through him we know not only with our head but also with our heart the realities of love, hope, and happiness. We can study love. We can define hope. We can analyze happiness. But they will be as painted fire—without warmth and consuming power—unless they are known in the experience of relationship. Love, hope, and happiness can be known in relationship with Jesus Christ. I'm not talking about some "Jesus who floats," who is out there in the air somewhere and will come floating into our lives. I'm talking about the Jesus of the Gospels—the one we meet as we bathe our minds with his teachings; as we hold our lives alongside his through prayer, word, and sacraments and let his love flow in and through us; and as we seek his face in the poor, the imprisoned, and the outcast. Yes, that is both truth and vital piety.

I knew a man through whom I experienced both a tough mind and a tender heart. I came to know him during my years as pastor in Oak Ridge, Tennessee. Dr. William Pollard was an eminent and well-respected physicist who helped to unlock the secrets of the atom. He was a towering intellect and a well-rounded scholar, researcher, administrator, and author. He also was an Episcopal priest. While serving as director of Oak Ridge Associated Universities, he was also part-time assistant rector of St. Stephens Episcopal Church. When I moved to Oak Ridge, Dr. Pollard was retired and in poor health. He had a long, painful battle with cancer which led to his death. But despite his suffering, Dr. Pollard was one of the most compassionate, humble, and sensitive persons I have ever known.

Some of my most treasured moments in that community were spent with Dr. Pollard. I can still see him taking his daily walk. I watched him from my office. Usually he would walk—with his shoulders erect and his head held high—to the church for morning prayers and the celebration of the Eucharist. Then he would make his way to the campus of Oak Ridge Associated Universities where he would confer with scientists and colleagues; or, he would stop at the library to read. Sometimes he would stop to chat with me or to bring me an article or a book. Every time he stopped to see me, I felt that I was in the presence of transcendence. His life challenged me to be more knowledgeable and more pious. He lived the tough mind and the tender heart. I know how he got the two together. He told me. It was through his relationship with Jesus Christ—his daily trips to the altar and the campus.

Keep these three thoughts in your head and your heart:

From Charles Wesley: "Let us unite the pair so long disjoined, knowledge and vital piety."[6]

From our Lord: "I am sending you out like sheep into the midst of wolves; so be wise as serpents and innocent as doves" (Matt. 10:16, NRSV); and

"If you continue in my word, you are truly my disciples; and you will know the truth, and the truth will make you free" (John 8:31-32, NRSV).

> *The God who made the world and everything in it, he who is Lord of heaven and earth, does not live in shrines made by human hands, nor is he served by human hands.*
>
> (*Acts 17:24-25a, NRSV*)

Acts 17:16-34

Tools for the Task

I grew up in a small rural community where everyone was either Baptist, Methodist, Presbyterian, or Pentecostal. The nearest Catholics and Jews lived in towns many miles from our community. Moslems, Hindus, and Buddhists lived in faraway lands. Occasionally something appeared in the weekly newspaper about these people, but we never met one of them. Everybody believed basically the same things. Religious differences centered mainly on sprinkling versus immersion as legitimate modes of baptism. Once-saved-always-saved Baptists countered Methodist preaching on backsliding, and the "formal" worship of the Presbyterians was viewed with suspicion by the Baptists, Methodists, and Pentecostals. The major ethical debates were about dancing, going to movies, and playing baseball on Sundays. The real sin took place in big cities. Ours was basically a serene, homogeneous community.

How different our worlds are today! Our daughter was graduated from a United Methodist university where approximately 40 percent of the students were Jewish and the campus ministry team included a Buddhist monk. One of her best friends was a black Moslem. Her roommate was Jewish. The faculty member for whom she worked was either an agnostic or atheist. The student body included representatives from more than one hundred countries. Speakers who visited the campus ranged from Jerry Falwell to Jesse Jackson, from Ronald

Reagan to George McGovern, and from Jahal Saddat to Phyllis Schafly. The ethical controversies included such issues as abortion, women's rights, genetic engineering, apartheid, homosexuality, disarmament, environmental justice, capital punishment, distribution of wealth, and medical care availability.

The contemporary world in which the church ministers and in which we seek to be faithful is more like that university campus than the rural community of my early years. Citizens of the remote villages of the world confront the diversity of values and complexity of issues through around-the-clock television broadcasts and the all-encompassing reach of modern bureaucracy. Even the most isolated and naive persons confront new ethical and moral dilemmas. Medical technology forces life or death decisions on the most unsuspecting families with such practices as screening genetics, prolonging life with heart and lung machines, donating and transplanting organs, and administering mind-altering and personality-changing drugs.

Explosions of knowledge confront persons of religious faith with serious questions. What do free will and sin mean if our behavior is more genetically determined than we have assumed? How do we hold on to a belief in a personal God in a vast universe of natural law? What does it mean to say "Christ is the way" when less than 25 percent of the world's people consider themselves Christians? These are but a few of the thorny new twists to some old questions. They must be addressed in light of the diverse challenges of living in this new world.

The apostle Paul found himself in a new world. His old world in which all questions had clear, precise answers had been shattered by his Damascus Road encounter with the Risen Christ. He had to sort out that experience and its revolutionary impact on his perception of himself and his tradition, to embark on a mission of divine mercy to the Gentiles whom he had considered to be beyond mercy, and to confront diverse peoples throughout Asia Minor.

Paul traveled to Athens, a university town and a center of Greek culture. New ideas, competing values, and diverse philosophies were the stock and trade of that metropolis. Sharing the gospel of God's redemptive action in Jesus Christ in that setting demanded all of the resources Paul could muster. Stock answers to difficult questions would not suffice. The new world required new tools. The Athenian intellectuals were more familiar with Zeus than with Yahweh—more familiar with Helen of Troy than with Miriam of the Exodus. Their heroes were Socrates, Plato, and Aristotle rather than Abraham, Isaac, and Jacob. So what tools did Paul bring to the task of dealing with the new world that was thrust upon him by his personal faith and the demands of the Athenian environment?

One of Paul's tools was his grounding in Hebrew Scripture. Paul, surrounded by a marketplace full of idols to foreign deities and learned philosophers ready to defend those deities, saw the situation through the lenses of the Scriptures. The Old Testament's emphasis on belief in one God and its warning against graven images shaped Paul's perception of and response to the Greek world. His grounding in Hebrew Scripture molded him and provided a framework for approaching a different culture. It provided a foundation upon which his new faith in Christ was built.

> *"The Bible remains the primary tool we use to approach the thorny issues of our time."*

The modern world, with its conflicting currents and diverse values, calls us to reexamine the primary tool for discerning God's presence and purposes: Scripture. The Bible has always been for us the primary witness to God's self-disclosure and redeeming activity. Our forebear John Wesley considered Scripture to be authoritative in matters of faith. He dealt with the whirling intellectual and social currents of eighteenth-century England with his faith firmly rooted in Scripture. He was so steeped in the Bible's stories and affirmations—in its language and concepts—that every personal and societal issue he faced was shaped by the Bible.

The Bible remains the primary tool we use to approach the thorny issues of our time. Its authority is rooted in its amazing ability to inspire, challenge, and guide those who take it seriously. Through its stories—its letters and sermons, its prayers and hymns, its parables and visions—God comes into our midst as one who transforms, guides, and sustains.

My fundamentalist heritage gave me a valuable gift. It indelibly etched in my soul the conviction that the Bible is God's Word. No, I am no longer a literalist. I do not read the Bible as if it were a fortune cookie or treat it as a transcript of God's dictation. But I have found that its message is timeless. Its analysis of the human condition and its prescription for the world's ills is a voice from beyond, breaking in upon the garbled noise of today's headlines. Reading the Bible and being confronted by its truth provides a foundation upon which to stand amid the shifting sands of mind-blowing new winds. It becomes a lens through which we view the kaleidoscopic issues thrust upon us by an increasingly secular world.

Although the Bible reflects the cultural limitations of its inspired peoples, its deepest truths transcend and challenge all cultures. Even though its stories reflect the images of a prescientific age, the God-given insights beneath the images are relevant in every age. From the creation stories, with their emphasis on the interrelatedness of all existence and the responsibility of human beings as caretakers and shepherds of creation, to the prophets' call and a social justice shaped by God's vision of shalom, the Bible challenges our limited visions and fragmented lives. From Jonah's judgment on narrow nationalism to John's dream of a new heaven and a new earth, the Bible expands our horizons to include all peoples. From Jesus' revelation of the nature and purpose of both God and true humanity to Paul's proclamation of salvation through grace alone, the Bible shapes, challenges, and transforms our life and the world with a Transcendent Word.

Another of Paul's tools was his tradition. As a respected Pharisee and member of the Sanhedrin, Paul was accustomed to interpreting and applying Jewish tradition to new situations. He knew the Torah and rabbinic literature. We should not be surprised, then, that Paul drew upon his tradition when confronting the alien gods and philosophies of the Greek world. It is obvious from Paul's speech to the philosophers that

> *"When confronted by personal tragedies . . . we must stay in touch with our Jerusalem."*

passages from the Wisdom of Solomon, from Isaiah 42, and from Psalm 74 were rumbling in his mind.

Paul not only drew upon his own tradition, but he also took seriously the tradition of the Athenians. He quoted from their philosophers and called attention to their heritage. He saw continuity and connecting points between his own traditions and those of the people whom he confronted in Athens.

A middle-aged woman, after years of addiction to alcohol and drugs, achieved sobriety and freedom. After two years without drugs or alcohol, she faced a terrible loss. Her husband and their only child were killed in an automobile accident. The temptation to numb the pain and to escape the horrible loss by reverting to old habits was almost overpowering. When asked how she was able to remain "clean," she said, "Along with the support of friends, I held on to what our preacher said on Pentecost Sunday. The disciples had faced a terrible loss. Their world had come apart. They were told to wait in Jerusalem, the center of their traditions and values. When my world came apart, I decided that the only way to survive would be to hold to my deeply rooted values. Otherwise, I would get blown away by life."

When confronted by personal tragedies as well as new challenges in the form of ideologies, life-styles, untried questions, and tough dilemmas, we must stay in touch with our Jerusalem—the center of our traditions and values. Otherwise, we may get blown away by unanswered and unanswerable questions, by earthshaking technological developments, and by unparalleled ethical dilemmas thrust upon us by this radically changing world. Our Jerusalem includes our historic creeds and liturgies, the great stories of our faith, the insights of the desert fathers and mothers, the hard-won victories of the reformers, the bloodstained examples of the martyrs, and the heartwarming sermons and hymns of the revivalists.

To the Athenians, Hebrew Scripture and tradition were insufficient resources. Quoting the Bible or reciting a historic creed would have received no more than an inquisitive nod or a sigh of indifference. Therefore, Paul had to call upon another tool in order to get a hearing and in order for the gospel to be relevant in a new setting.

> *"God is present in and with every person and in all of life."*

Paul met the Athenians at the point of their experience. He acknowledged their longings for transcendence. Rather than put down their experience, the apostle affirmed their genuine search for the ultimate. He accepted the validity of the insights of their traditions and heroes. Rather than introduce the Athenians to God, as though they had no experience of the Divine, Paul named that which they had experienced but had labeled *unknown*.

Herein lies a critical affirmation for us as we seek to be faithful to God in a pluralistic world and as we evaluate the conflicting voices that compete for our attention. *God is present in and with every person and in all of life.* God is not present with some and absent from others. All persons experience the reality of God in whom "we live and move and have our being" (Acts 17:28, NRSV). Not all persons, however, know that it is God whom they experience.

In Jesus Christ, God has claimed all of life as the realm of God's presence—including smelly stables, foreboding crosses, peaceful hillsides, and empty tombs. All persons have been claimed as members of a loving household and as birth-givers of divine grace—including unmarried pregnant servant girls, uncultured fishermen, abused women of the street, outcast Samaritans, Roman soldiers, unclean lepers, and dying thieves. The research laboratory and corporate boardroom, the surgical room and classroom, the United Nations and United States Congress—all are realms wherein God is at work. Scientists and surgeons, professors and corporate executives, ambassadors and congress members, homemakers and factory workers, police officers and social workers, homosexuals and heterosexuals, divorced persons and married persons, Arabs and Jews, Protestants and Catholics, atheists and believers—everyone experiences the reality and presence of God!

It remains our task to be open to that Divine Presence in us and in others and to hold the common experience of all against the criteria of Scripture and tradition. God often comes to us from the experiences of those whom we assume do not know God. After all, Cyrus, the pagan king of Persia, is called "God's Anointed" by Isaiah. Whether Cyrus intended it to be so or not, God acted in him to free the Hebrews from Babylonian captivity.

All experience, however, is to be evaluated in light of the redemptive, reconciling love known in Jesus Christ. The reality of which Christ is the incarnation is agape love. The command to love remains at the center of what it means to be faithful to God. The modern world places many complex realities before us, but the fundamental question we must persistently raise is this: How and where is love to be expressed? There God is!

Paul didn't stop with the Athenians' unnamed experience. He connected their experience to the Risen Christ, who is the shape and source of authentic love. Scripture, tradition, experience—these were resources used by Paul as he stood in the Areopagus. But Paul had another vital tool or criterion: *reason*.

> *"Reason . . . can be a fertile field in which the seeds of eternal truth grow to maturity."*

The Athenian philosophers worshiped at the altar of reason, so it was there that Paul met them. Drawing upon the insights of Stoic and Epicurean philosophers, Paul attempted to connect these curious products of Greek culture to the God made known in Jesus Christ. Paul told the Athenians, "From one ancestor he made all nations to inhabit the whole earth" (Acts 17:26, NRSV). Paul then quoted their own thinkers and poets: "In him we live and move and have our being. . . . For we too are his offspring" (Acts 17:28, NRSV).

The human mind can be a factory for the production of idols, but it also can be a scalpel by which cancerous idols are removed from the body of Christ, the church. Reason, motivated by love and marching under the banner of faith, can be a fertile field in which the seeds of eternal truth grow to maturity. In 1768, John Wesley wrote in a sharply worded reply to a theologian at Cambridge University, "To renounce reason is to renounce religion. . . . [for] all irrational religion is false religion."[1]

An illustrious physicist I know is typical of many in our society. His boyhood years were spent in a very rigid church in which questioning was considered to be a sign of inadequate faith. He left the church and became an agnostic. Yet, he found the universe shrouded in mystery and wonder. He made his way to worship. In the liturgy he found a vehicle for expressing his sense of praise and adoration toward an indefinite reality he called God. We had many conversations, and from him I learned much. I introduced him to process theology and the writings of John Cobb, Charles Hartshorne, and Marjorie Suchocki. He found in these theologians a challenge to his mind that enabled him to read the Bible with fresh openness and to recite the creeds with new integrity. Reason was an avenue of God's presence.

I received a letter from an eleven-year-old member of the congregation. Here is part of the letter:

> In the Bible it says that several days after making the earth God made Adam and Eve. But in science, it says that no one lived before the dinosaurs or while they were living. How could dinosaurs have lived for millions of years before people if God made Adam and Eve seven days after the earth was made? . . . I hope you won't be mad at me, but sometimes I have trouble believing . . . but I still believe in God.

This young friend of mine whose name is Adam lost his father when he was nine. He is bright and articulate. Somewhere he got the notion that to use his mind, which inevitably results in questioning, is outside the mainstream of faith. On the contrary, through reason he and countless others can glorify the God who is the source of all truth.

Church Street Church is located in downtown Knoxville, Tennessee. To the west is the University of Tennessee campus, with its diverse community of 25,000 people. On the north boundary of the church's property is the site of the 1982 World's Fair, which now consists of a park, restaurants, an amphitheater, and the Sunsphere. To the east are offices, banks, federal and local courthouses, hotels, and the complex housing one of the country's fastest-growing communications offices, Whittle Communications. The river on our south carries the barges and boats southward. Hundreds of people pass by the church every day—old and young, rich and poor, educated and illiterate, Christians and Jews, Hindus and Moslems, atheists and agnostics, the sheltered and the homeless. The church is in the center of a microcosm of the modern world. How will Church Street Church proclaim and live the gospel in a world of diverse philosophies, conflicting life-styles, overwhelming needs, and unparalleled challenges?

Scripture, tradition, reason, and experience are avenues by which God comes to us from that world out there beyond our gothic walls, and they are means by which God transforms that world through us.

Part Two:
Sermons on Our Doctrinal Beliefs

*For by grace you have been saved through faith,
and this is not your own doing; it is the gift of God.*
(*Ephesians 2:8, NRSV*)

Ephesians 2:1-10

Transforming Grace

A teenage girl was brought by her mother to see the pastor. The beautiful young woman was depressed and was becoming increasingly rebellious. She was an honor student. She played on the school soccer team, sang in the chorus, and was a member of the drama club. Her courses included advanced English, advanced calculus, and advanced biology. Her father was a revered scientist, a skilled craftsman, and a highly respected citizen. Her mother, a college graduate, worked part time and managed the household.

Subsequent visits to the pastor revealed a scared and anxious young woman. She was afraid of making less than an "A" in her courses. She feared losing on the soccer field. She wanted to win the lead part in the school drama. Added to all of this was her desperate fear of not scoring high enough on the SAT to get into a prestigious university. Her self-esteem was low and her self-worth was contingent upon her ranking with her peers and her ability to fulfill both her own and her parents' exceptionally high expectations.

This young woman is but one of the countless folks in our society who suffer from a secular form of legalism, or works righteousness. Few people seem to worry about religious obedience. Fear of transgressing divine laws or violating religious rules is not the motivator that it once was. Not many of us try to earn our salvation, our wholeness, our worth, or our well-being by religious obedience. So legalism, as traditionally understood, is of little threat to the modern church.

However, our fear of failure, our anxiety about measuring up and fitting in, drives us to find peace through achieving, winning, accumulating, and knowing. We compulsively seek to prove our worth, establish our identity, and secure our destiny through such secular works as SAT scores, academic degrees, financial success, social prominence, athletic accomplishments, and countless other acts of obedience to the prevailing culture. Guilt, shame, stress, low self-esteem, anxiety about today and tomorrow, neglected relationships, and poor health are but a few of the destructive results of our secular version of salvation by works.

In eighteenth-century England there lived a man who pursued salvation—a sense of wholeness and peace with himself, with others, and with God. He tried scholarly avenues by becoming an avid student and later a faculty member at prestigious Oxford University. He pursued his place in life through religious zeal by becoming a priest in the Anglican church and a missionary to America. His search for salvation took him in the direction of social action as he visited prisoners, tutored the poor, and spoke against evils such as slavery and the abuse of alcohol. But his compulsive attempts to redeem himself, to secure himself, and to prove himself before God did not bring peace, or a sense of "home-ness" with himself, the world, and God. He sought inner assurance of his own worth and identity, but it eluded him.

Then, on May 24, 1738, John Wesley recorded that while attending a meeting of a religious society that was studying Martin Luther's commentary on Romans, "I felt my heart strangely warmed. I felt I did trust in Christ, Christ alone for salvation: And an assurance was given me, that he had taken away *my* sins, even *mine*, and saved *me* from the law of sin and death."[1] Wesley's "heartwarming experience" was preceded by thirty-five years of attempting to earn worth, acceptance, and God's favor. And the struggle continued. Yet, Wesley came to appropriate what he had heard others preach and what he himself had preached; that is, we are saved by grace through faith.

Grace became a major emphasis of Wesley's preaching, and it has been a distinctive note in our Wesleyan heritage. It is a note that needs to be sounded with renewed clarity in a world that proclaims salvation through achieving, accumulating, winning, knowing, and doing. Wesley's emphasis on threefold grace speaks relevantly to the contemporary mind-set.

> *"We are surrounded by gifts that we could never merit or create."*

First, there is prevenient grace. According to Wesley, prevenient grace is present in creation which is a gift, in our families which we did not choose but which we inherit, in the church's word and sacraments which are gifts, and in a conscience which drives us to do what is right. We are surrounded by gifts that we could never merit or create. These "natural" gifts are prevenient grace—God's unmerited love available to all. These gifts are intimations of a Transcendent Love. They whet our appetites for more. These gifts point us toward a grace that transforms all that is.

For Wesley, prevenient grace was the porch of religion. Some people live out their days on the porch. They experience God's grace at the edge, out on the periphery. We do not disparage such porch dwellers. Indeed, becoming aware of wonderful gifts that one can enjoy on the porch is itself an act of grace.

Paul Tournier, the Swiss psychotherapist, said that "there comes a day when a man [person] understands that all is of grace, that the whole world is a gift of God, a completely generous gift. . . . We see each flower, each drop of water, each minute of our life as a gift of God."[2] That is prevenient grace . . . but there is more!

There also is *justifying* grace. Justifying grace, which may come suddenly or gradually, is the assurance that we are forgiven daughters and sons of God. Justification is being claimed as children of God—the infinitely, unconditionally loved children of God. That is what Wesley experienced at

> *"Identity, self-worth, and security rooted in God's unconditional love . . . set us free to be who we are."*

Aldersgate Street. He felt claimed and forgiven by God. He personally accepted God's redemptive acts in Jesus Christ. He came to a new way of viewing himself. His worth and identity were contained in whom he belonged to, not in his accomplishments or achievements.

There is freedom in justifying grace. This self-acceptance based on God's acceptance has been a long time coming to me. As one who has sought to escape the dungeon of feelings of inferiority through academic achievement, professional competency, and religious devotion, I can testify to the liberating power of an identity based on what God has done rather than on what I must do. Identity, self-worth, and security rooted in God's unconditional love and God's claim upon us set us free to be who we are, and who we are is nothing less than daughters and sons of the Eternal One whose name and nature is Love.

If prevenient grace is the porch of vital religion, then justifying grace is the doorway. The door always has a welcome sign on it. It is a doorway into a new identity, a new family home, and a new future. Just as some may live their lives on the porch, so also may others get stuck in the doorway. They assume that entrance through the door is the end of the journey. Consequently, they spend their days either standing in the doorway, reveling narcissistically in their relationship with God, or staying close to the entrance in a desperate attempt to hold onto the freshness of entering the doorway for the first time.

> *"Sanctifying grace is God's unending pursuit of Christlikeness in us."*

Wesley, therefore, placed an emphasis on a third dimension of grace: sanctification. Sanctification is the endless exploration of the rest of the house. It is nothing less than the restoration of the divine image in us. Sanctifying grace is God's unending pursuit of Christlikeness in us. It is going on toward perfection—being made perfect in love. Sanctifying grace is living the full range of God's claim upon us, with gratitude, until all of life reflects the beauty of God's peace—shalom.

There is a legend of a prince who had a crooked back. He wanted above everything else to be straight and tall, in accordance with his own image of the worthy prince. He had a sculptor to carve a statue of the prince standing tall and erect—the prince as he should have been. When the statue was completed, it was placed in the palace garden. Several times each day the prince would stand before the image of the prince. There he would contemplate himself as he would like to be. Eventually, the people began to notice a change in the prince. He was becoming tall and erect. He was growing into the likeness of his ideal image.

Our ideal image has been sculpted in Jesus of Nazareth. He is God's goal for us. It is his likeness that is stamped all over the rooms of this house of grace. We seek to follow him toward the kingdom that God is bringing. That is sanctifying grace.

As we follow the Christ along the corridors of God's "many mansions" (John 14:2, KJV), we stumble and fall. We lose our way time and again. But once more there is the door with the welcome sign on it. Again we claim our identity as daughters and sons of God—brothers and sisters of the Christ—and we continue our journey toward that city not made with human hands.

"For by grace you have been saved through faith, and this is not your own doing; it is the gift of God" (Eph. 2:8, NRSV). By grace we have been saved. By grace we are saved. By grace we shall be saved. Thanks be to God for the unspeakable gift of prevenient, justifying, and sanctifying grace!

> *I press on toward the goal for the prize of the heavenly call of God in Christ Jesus.*
>
> (*Philippians 3:14, NRSV*)

Matthew 5:43-48; Philippians 3:12-21

Going on to Perfection

The questions have been asked of every United Methodist preacher for 250 years. John Wesley asked them of his "local preachers" and class leaders, all of whom were lay persons. Therefore, they are appropriate questions for all who call themselves United Methodists.

Here are the questions: 1) Have you faith in Christ? 2) Are you going on to perfection? 3) Do you expect to be made perfect in love in this life? 4) Are you earnestly striving after it?[1]

I'll admit that I flinch when these questions are asked by the bishop during the examination of ministerial candidates. When they were addressed to me twenty-five years ago, I mumbled yes, but I really didn't comprehend the depth of the questions or the significance of my answer. I suspect that we contemporary United Methodists have strayed from our Wesleyan path at this point more than any other.

> *"Wesley considered the doctrine of Christian perfection . . . to be the distinctive emphasis of Methodism."*

The call to holy living—the pursuit of perfection—was a consistent theme in early Methodist preaching. It was the driving vision of John Wesley's life. On June 22, 1763, he wrote to Henry Venn, "What I want is holiness of heart and life."[2] In fact, Wesley considered the doctrine of Christian perfection— or holiness of heart and life, or sanctification—to be the distinctive emphasis of Methodism. He wrote in September 1790, "This doctrine is the grand depositum which God has lodged with the people called Methodists; and for the sake of propagating this chiefly He [God] appeared to have raised us up."[3] He felt so strongly about its importance that he wrote two months later, "If we can prove that any of our Local Preachers or Leaders, either directly or indirectly, speak against it, let him be a Local Preacher or Leader no longer."[4] Wesley was convinced that the spread of Methodism depended upon preaching Christian perfection. "Wherever this is not done," he wrote in his journal, "the believers grow dead and cold."[5]

Although non-Methodists and Methodists alike have found the doctrine puzzling and fraught with dangers, Wesley warned that to neglect Christian perfection is to deny Scripture. Christian perfection is clearly at the heart of Jesus' preaching as he summons disciples to "be perfect, therefore, as your heavenly Father is perfect" (Matt. 5:48, NRSV), a text on which Wesley preached at least eighteen times. Furthermore, the Epistle to the Hebrews reads, "Therefore let us go on toward perfection" (Heb. 6:1, NRSV), which was the text of at least fifty sermons written by Wesley.

Let us acknowledge right now that the Bible and Wesley's call to the pursuit of perfection is fraught with dangers and misinterpretations. The call to holy living can provide a theological underpinning for a crippling psychological compulsiveness. Perfectionism plagues many of us and robs us of the holiness and happiness that Wesley held as God's goal for all people. Our dogged attempts to be perfect, to excel in everything and to be all that we can be, can wind us up and drive us mad. We all know persons who never can enjoy anything less than perfection; nothing and no one ever meets their impossible expectations.

If we are not careful, this challenge to go on to perfection can put us on the pathway of self-righteousness. Holy living can become so narrowly defined that it merely matches our achievements. A list of do's and don'ts is substituted for a dynamic covenantal relationship with God in Christ, which is the heart of discipleship. Soon we are judging ourselves and others by our rule-oriented perfection. Feelings of either smug self-righteousness or self-defeating compulsiveness result.

Jesus was not calling us to a flawless life—no mistakes, no errors, no weaknesses. Neither the Bible nor Wesley hold before us mortals a world in which anything less than an "A" is a failure. God is not a perfectionist who accepts only anthems sung perfectly and lives lived flawlessly.

Neither does the call to perfection imply the loss of the consciousness of sin. In fact, perfection is paradoxical. The closer one gets to it, the more one is aware of his or her failure to achieve it. Simon Peter's plea reflects the self-awareness of the person closest to the one who was the very incarnation of perfection: "Go away from me, Lord, for I am a sinful man!" (Luke 5:8, NRSV) The nearer we get to authentic perfection, the greater is our consciousness of our own imperfection. So what does it mean to be going on to perfection?

> *"Christian perfection is nothing less than the total restoration of the divine image in us."*

In Wesley's preaching, Christian perfection means the same as sanctification, holiness of heart and life, or perfect love. In Wesley's own words, "Perfection is another name for universal holiness—inward and outward righteousness—holiness of life arising from holiness of heart."[6] Christian perfection is nothing less than the total restoration of the divine image in us. In the ancient world, a ruler or king often would erect statues in the king's likeness throughout the provinces. Those images of the king enabled the citizens to remember to whom they belonged and helped people to recognize the king.

59

God created us as reflections of God's own nature and character. Our identity and our destiny are rooted in our potential as images of the one to whom we belong. As daughters and sons of the Holy One, we are to be holy. As offspring of the Loving One, we are to be loving. That is our goal! That is God's promise!

Bishop Earl Ledden told this story about Phillips Brooks, a great preacher of the nineteenth century. Rev. Brooks used to stop each day on the street corner in Boston to buy a newspaper from a vendor. One day as the kind and eloquent preacher walked away from the newspaper stand, glancing at the headlines, the vendor said to another customer, "Whenever I see that man, I think of God." In the vendor's mind, Phillips Brooks exemplified what the Bible and Wesley mean by perfection—the fulfillment of the image of God.

The key phrase in Matthew 5:48 is "as your heavenly Father is perfect" (NRSV). Likewise, the Levitical Code affirms, "You shall be holy, for I the Lord your God am holy" (Lev. 19:2, NRSV). In his sermon entitled "Circumcision of the Heart," Wesley proclaimed that the goal of Christian living is "being so 'renewed in the image of our mind' as to be 'perfect, as our Father in heaven is perfect.' "[7]

The quality of divine perfection, however, is not measurable by some objective standard. To reflect the image of God is to love God with one's whole being and to love our neighbors as ourselves. Wesley said, "This is the sum of Christian perfection: it is all comprised in that one word, love."[8] Jesus' challenge and promise, "Be perfect, therefore, as your heavenly Father is perfect" (Matt. 5:48, NRSV), concludes a description of a love that reaches the bounds of God's love, a love broad enough to include enemies. It is in the context of Jesus' call to a life-style of undying, inclusive love that Jesus calls for perfection. It is perfect love that characterizes Christian perfection.

One of my most respected and challenging mentors was Dr. Harold DeWolf, one of United Methodism's great intellects and teachers. His keen mind was matched by a magnanimous spirit and sensitive social conscience. Among the many students influenced by him was Dr. Martin Luther King, Jr. Shortly after Dr. DeWolf's retirement from his position as Dean of Wesley

Theological Seminary, I had the privilege of having him spend a weekend in the church I was serving. His very presence spoke of the love and justice he summoned the congregation to embody. When we were having dinner together one evening, he said this about an acquaintance of ours: "He is an example of the fact that the final work of grace is that it makes one graceful, full of grace." Dr. DeWolf was one in whom the grace and love of God were embodied. What he said about another, he unknowingly reflected in himself: a life full of grace. That is Christian perfection.

Such perfection does not remove the reality of sin; it does, however, remove the desire to sin. It celebrates an optimism that God's grace is powerful enough to work in us what God requires of us. This brings us to the final, critical question: From whence does this perfection in love come?

> *"Christian perfection is no achievement at all. . . . It is a gift."*

Certainly, perfection in love does not result from our efforts. No one can boast of having achieved it. Rolling up our sleeves, mustering our emotional and spiritual resources, and trying harder will not get us to the destination. Harry Emerson Fosdick was right: "He [Jesus] was deliberately presenting [in the Sermon on the Mount] a way of life so demanding that no legalism could define it, no unredeemed heart practice it, no saint perfectly fulfill it."[9]

Christian perfection grows out of a relationship. It is no achievement at all. It is a gift, a gift wrapped in a relationship with Jesus the Christ. For Wesley, perfection describes a relationship more than it defines a code of conduct. To be going on to perfection means to have faith in Christ. That is, it means to trust Christ not only as the one who forgives us but also as the one who transforms us with a new heart of love and grace.

The call to perfection is a command and a promise. John

Wesley preached that all of God's commandments are "covered" with God's promises. God does not require what God is unwilling to accomplish for us. The summons to go on to perfection is covered with the promise, "My grace is sufficient for you" (II Cor. 12:8, NRSV). Its meaning and promise are summarized in the Epistle of John: "Beloved, we are God's children now; what we will be has not yet been revealed. What we do know is this: when he is revealed, we will be like him, for we will see him as he is" (I John 3:2, NRSV).

We take on the nature, the likeness, of that which means most to us. A son or daughter unconsciously imitates his or her parents. We take on the qualities of our heroes. Love transforms us into the likeness of the beloved. Christian perfection is nothing less than the process of taking on the image of the Christ, whose love moves us to love.

Many of you know the story of Toyohiko Kagawa, the Japanese humanitarian who spent his life among the poor of Japan.[10] His early life was rather turbulent and traumatic. He was born into a wealthy family, but his parents died when he was a young child. After living on the Kagawa farm until age eleven, he was sent away to school. His eagerness to learn English took him to the home of Presbyterian missionaries Harry Myers and Charles Logan.

Though the young student thought the missionaries were rather foolish in their religious ways and teachings, he went to them because they spoke and taught English. When he was learning to read and speak English, he first read the story of Jesus. He was struck by Jesus' compassion for the poor and outcast and Jesus' love for his enemies. He could not believe that such a good man had been killed. Kagawa was captured by admiration for Jesus. One day before leaving the missionaries' study, he knelt and uttered his first Christian prayer: "O God, make me like Christ."[11]

Much to his family's dismay, Kagawa was baptized. He continued to read the Gospels, as well as the writings of Thoreau and Tolstoy. He made a commitment to pacifism—not a popular philosophy in Japan, who was at war with Russia. One day a group of students attacked him, attempting to provoke him into violence. They beat him severely, but Kagawa prayed the prayer of the one whose likeness he had prayed to become: "Father, forgive them" (Luke 23:34, NRSV). The boys walked away in silence, convinced of the depth of Kagawa's commitment and love. One of the boys later became a minister.

Kagawa went on to study theology, but his commitment was to the poor, among whom he lived his entire life. He worked for social change and was consulted by international agencies concerned with economic reform and justice. He was a vital force in the reconstruction of post-war Japan.

What accounts for Kagawa's magnanimous, compassionate, and holy life? It was the prayer that he prayed in the home of his missionary friends: "O God, make me like Christ." He was molded and shaped by his relationship with the loving and transforming Christ. That is going on to perfection.

Charles Wesley wrote a poem entitled "The Promise of Sanctification." Its twenty-eight verses express the Wesleyan understanding and vision of perfection. It was circulated by John Wesley with his first edition of his sermon "On Perfection." I close with two verses as our prayer:

> Give me a new, a perfect heart,
> From doubt, and fear, and sorrow free;
> The mind which was in Christ impart,
> And let my spirit cleave to thee.
>
> Now let me gain perfection's height!
> Now let me into nothing fall!
> Be less than nothing in my sight,
> And feel that Christ is all in all.[12]

> *You shall love the Lord your God with all your heart, and with all your soul, and with all your mind. . . . You shall love your neighbor as yourself.*
> (*Matthew 22:37, 39, NRSV*)

Matthew 22:34-40

Being Saved Isn't Enough

"Knowing Jesus as your personal savior is all that matters," says the elegantly dressed, carefully groomed, properly postured young engineer and mother of two sons. She is a member of a Sunday school class that is discussing "what it means to be a Christian." Raising her head and chin slightly, Marge says firmly, "Being saved is enough."

There follows an uncomfortable silence born of embarrassment and judgment. Clearing his throat and looking straight ahead in order to avoid eye contact, an administrator in the local welfare department replies, "What really matters is what we do for others. After all, Jesus said that in the end we will be judged on the basis of our feeding the hungry, clothing the naked, and visiting the imprisoned and the sick." Gaining confidence from the nodding heads around him, Frank continues, "No, what really matters is changing society."

Marge and Frank are representatives of a long-existing struggle in the church to determine the most important dimension of discipleship. This struggle goes all the way back to the Bible itself. In the Bible God is portrayed as a shepherd who goes out in search of one lost lamb. Upon finding it, the Divine Shepherd cradles the lamb in compassionate arms and restores it to the fold (Luke 15:3-5). Likewise, God is compared to a diligent homemaker who moves all the furniture, picks up all the rugs, and looks in every nook and cranny for one lost coin

64

(Luke 15:6-8). But God is also described as one who demands justice and one who is the liberator of slaves, the creator of a new heaven and a new earth, the transformer of structures and societies, and the ruler of peoples, nations, and communities.

A religious leader who was schooled in the law and was meticulous in his personal observance of it questioned Jesus about this issue. He asked, "Teacher, which commandment in the law is the greatest?" Jesus responded, " 'You shall love the Lord your God with all your heart, and with all your soul, and with all your mind.' This is the greatest and first commandment. And a second is like it: 'You shall love your neighbor as yourself' " (Matt. 22:37-39, NRSV).

Personal assurance and *social witness*—these are the terms in our Wesleyan heritage that describe the two dimensions of discipleship. Being saved and societal transformation are both necessary components of authentic faith. Marge and Frank need each other!

> *"God in Christ Jesus lays claim upon us, cleanses us from a guilt-ridden past, and sets us free. . . ."*

Much of the Bible, church history, reason, and experience come down on the side of Marge. Those who have had an experience of being claimed, forgiven, and set free by an assurance of divine love would testify, "Being saved is all that matters." This would be true especially for those experiencing the warm afterglow of a heartwarming conversion. Indeed, the promises of the gospel and our own experiences, perhaps such as John Wesley's Aldersgate renewal, validate that God in Christ Jesus lays claim upon us, cleanses us from a guilt-ridden past, and sets us free to be sons and daughters of the Eternal God. For much of his adult life, John Wesley longed for the personal assurance that he had been redeemed, reconciled, and liberated by the saving acts of God in Jesus Christ. The assurance of salvation from sin was a dominant theme of his preaching as he proclaimed God's prevenient, justifying, and sanctifying grace to the masses of eighteenth-century England.

Many of us are the beneficiaries of that message proclaimed by the Methodist evangelists of a former generation. I vividly recall my experience as an eleven-year-old child attending a revival in a small white-frame Methodist church in upper East Tennessee. The evangelist graphically described the need of every person to accept Jesus Christ as their personal Savior. He told us that Christ died on our behalf and wants us to feel loved and forgiven. I made my way down the aisle as the congregation sang "I Surrender All." I was joined by my Sunday school teacher who put his arms around me. The members of the congregation filed by, hugging me and sharing my tears of joy. Oh, my understanding of that experience is different now than it was that autumn evening almost forty years ago. It was neither the first nor the last time I experienced God's grace—nor was it my "conversion." But it was a wonderful catalyst through which I received an assurance of forgiveness—the first fruits of a growing new identity as a child of God.

Christ came to save persons from all that enslaves, destroys, alienates, and distorts the divine image. We have been forgiven. We are children of God, *now*. We are the prodigals welcomed home, the treasure recovered, the lost sheep restored to the fold.

> *"God not only saves us from, but God also saves us for."*

Personal assurance of being saved, transformed, set free— that is gospel, good news. But it also can be, as Harry Emerson Fosdick said a generation ago, the supreme appeal to our selfishness. Being saved can become a form of pious narcissism, which causes us to clutch and hoard our faith as a child clutches a stuffed teddy bear or a teenager parades a new sports car as if to say "Look what I have that you don't." Being saved isn't enough. Marge must listen to Frank, or else she may spend her days revelling in her own relationship with God while ignoring the primary focus of God's attention: the transformation of the world—the cosmos. "For God so loved the world [*cosmos,* not only individual persons] that he gave his only Son" (John 3:16, NRSV).

God not only saves us *from,* but God also saves us *for.* Abraham and Sarah weren't called by Yahweh so that they could boast of a new status in their old age. Yahweh called them *for* the creation of a new people, a new covenantal community. Yahweh didn't appear to Moses out of the burning bush to give Moses peace of mind—tranquility of spirit—so that he could spend his days on the slopes tending Jethro's sheep and dreaming of heaven. Rather, because of Yahweh's call, Moses banged on Pharaoh's palace door with a demanding message: "Yahweh says you'd better let my people go." And Moses spent the rest of his days leading a murmuring people through the wilderness toward a promised land that he saw only from a distance.

I was in seminary when I fully realized that being saved wasn't enough—that I had been saved *for* as well as *from.* The year was 1964. I was taking a class on the church and the community. The professor was Dr. Haskell Miller. The assignment included a visit to the ghettos of Washington, D.C. We were to interview residents regarding their understanding of and attitude toward a church located in the neighborhood. One elderly man sat on the steps of the tenement building. Within sight was the spire of a Methodist church.

"What do you know about that church?" I asked as I pointed toward the shining steeple.

"I don't know nothing about it, 'cept it's there," replied the longtime resident of the run-down tenement.

"Do you know of anything the church does in the community?" I asked.

His poignant answer pierced my smugly pious life like a prophet's word: "They don't do nothin' down there but have church." He could hear them sing on Sunday morning, "Blessed assurance, Jesus is mine." Then he would watch as they drove back to their cloistered lives, away from the torment of their Sunday-morning-only neighbors.

While still a seminary student, I served as the pastor of two small churches in Montgomery County, Maryland. They had a combined membership of 150 persons. Located between the two churches was a small Methodist church—one of two churches served by a man who became my friend. The congregations he served totaled approximately four hundred persons. He taught me a lot about the church and its failure to strike a balance between personal assurance and social transformation.

My friend, who was in his mid-fifties, had a master's degree from Harvard. He had been a pastor for thirty years. I was in my early twenties and had a bachelor's degree from East Tennessee State University. I had no experience as a pastor, yet my salary was two hundred dollars more than his salary. Why the difference? He was black. It was no longer possible for me to assume that being saved was enough when the church itself practiced injustice in its institutional structure.

The slums of England, the exploitation of children in the factories and mines of England, the buying and selling of human beings as slaves, the deplorable conditions of British prisons, and the disparity between the haves and the have-nots of his time reminded John Wesley that being saved isn't enough. He preached personal assurance, but not at the expense of social transformation. Let us remember that Wesley challenged widely condoned sins such as slavery, which he considered to be one of the most heinous, despicable evils ever perpetrated by human beings. He spoke out against the distilling industry, against unjust taxation, and against opulent living.

Wesley's refusal to properly acknowledge social rankings and his call for an equality based on a common need for the grace of God created a stir among some of "the rich and famous." The Duchess of Buckingham wrote to Lady Huntington:

> Their doctrines [the Methodists] are most repulsive and tinctured with impertinence and disrespect toward their superiors, in perpetually endeavoring to level all ranks and doing away with all distinctions. It is monstrous to be told that you have a heart as sinful as the common wretches that crawl the earth. This is highly offensive and insulting.[1]

God raised the people called Methodists, according to Wesley, "to reform the nation, particularly the Church, and to spread

> *"Love for God is inextricably tied to love for neighbor."*

scriptural holiness over the land."[2] This was the propelling vision of the Wesleyan revival. It was a two-pronged gospel of personal assurance and social witness. Wesley never preached holiness apart from social holiness. That message—proclaimed in the fields, nurtured in class meetings, and lived out in factories, mines, schools, and shops—transformed the soul of eighteenth-century England.

Loving God and being loved by God should permeate all of one's life. Otherwise, faith dissolves into a pious placebo. Love for God is inextricably tied to love for neighbor. In Luke's account, the lawyer who asked Jesus about the essence of discipleship learned that love for neighbor involves one with all kinds of people—such as despised Samaritans and wounded folks lying in ditches—and in all kinds of tasks—including retrieving those wounded folks from the allies and gutters; providing shelter, food, and medical care; and making the Jericho roads safe for travel (Luke 15:25-37).

Yes, Marge, being saved is good news. Yes, Frank, feeding the hungry, clothing the naked, caring for the homeless, and visiting the sick and imprisoned are at the heart of discipleship. The two belong together. Only being saved or only doing good is not enough. The gospel is both personal assurance and social witness—love of God and love of neighbor.

Luke 16:1-13

On Being Two-Thirds Wesleyan

A speaker at a civic club had been asked to share reasons for his success as an entrepreneur. My attention increased when he attributed his extraordinary financial success to the philosophy of John Wesley. He said, "Wesley said that we are to earn all we can and save all we can. If we earn all we can and save all we can, then we can invest in new and profitable ventures."

The speaker was, at best, only two-thirds Wesleyan. *Earn all you can* and *save all you can* are two of the three basic points of John Wesley's famous sermon entitled "The Use of Money." The critical emphasis of Wesley's understanding of stewardship is made in the third point: *give all you can.*

Wesley observed in 1789 that the Methodists of eighteenth-century England had ignored the third point of his sermon, just as the civic club speaker of the twentieth century did. In fact, Wesley contended that the primary reason for the ineffectiveness of the Methodists lay in their failure to give. He observed:

> Of the three rules which are laid down . . . you may find many that observe the first rule, namely, 'Gain all you can.' You may find a few that observe the second, 'Save all you can.' But how many have you found that observe the third rule, 'Give all you can'? Have you reason to believe that five hundred of these are to be found among fifty thousand Methodists? And yet nothing can be more plain than that all who observe the two first rules without the third will be twofold more the children of hell than ever they were before.[1]

70

For Wesley, Christianity has within it seeds of its own ineffectiveness. Frugality and diligence characterize true scriptural Christianity, and they in turn "beget pride, love of the world, and every temper that is destructive of [to] Christianity."[2] Wesley observed that Methodists had prospered by practicing the virtues of diligence and frugality. He warned, "It is an observation which admits of few exceptions, that nine in ten of these [who had become wealthy] decreased in grace in the same proportion as they increased in wealth."[3]

Wesley's warnings of the dangers of wealth and the misuse of money echo those of Jesus. Both Jesus and Wesley seemed to be afraid of money, for it tends to do something destructive to the human soul. And yet when viewed from the perspective of a steward, wealth can be a means of fulfilling God's purpose for creation. Just as Jesus had much to say about wealth, so also Wesley preached on stewardship more than any theme other than grace and holy living. Perhaps no sermon has more relevance for contemporary Methodists than Wesley's sermon based on Luke 16:1-13, "The Use of Money."

In an era when United Methodists are predominantly middle class and the doctrine of acquisitiveness is a central tenet of civil religion, we would do well to ask the question Wesley raised more than two hundred years ago: What can we do to prevent wealth from destroying our very souls? His answer represents a radical form of stewardship rooted in the New Testament and the teaching and example of our Lord.

First, *gain all you can*. Do any of us need to be urged to gain all that we can? Is not acquisitiveness and the profit motive the driving force of our economy as well as our value system? Lest we assume that Wesley was providing rationale for rampant acquisitiveness, let us note that his emphasis was on earning all one can within the guidelines and restraints of an ethic based on love of God and compassion for others. His sermon could never be used properly as a cheer for unbridled profit-seeking and acquisition. In fact, the emphasis in his sermon is the restrictions on the pursuit of wealth.

How one gains wealth is a crucial test of stewardship, according to Wesley. Profit at the expense of health, integrity, honesty, and the well-being of others is prohibited. Proper gain

71

> *"The failure to gain all that we can as participants in God's attempts to secure wholeness for creation is a collective sin."*

is to be derived from exercising one's partnership with the Creator God who is ever laboring to gain the wholeness and well-being of creation. Gaining all you can, therefore, is to be understood as participation in God's efforts to heal and redeem all of creation, not as permission to "feather the nest" and increase one's own opulence.

A researcher went to her pastor with a moral dilemma. She had been devoting her research to a better understanding of the effects of the environment on the human body. Funds for her research were severely cut, and she was directed by her company to move to the weapons division where she would participate in weaponry research. She said, "I became a scientist in order to help the human family. I can't spend my life in developing that which seeks to destroy people." She was caught in one of the modern world's most painful stewardship dilemmas—profiting from that which threatens, harms, and destroys others. Gain from alcohol and drug abuse, weapons production, and environmental destruction are modern threats to Wesley's challenge of a stewardship that gains from adding to the healing and health of all creation.

None of us can claim innocence or speak with self-righteousness. As Americans, we profit from the exploitation of poor nations of the world. Our comfortable, wasteful life-style is gained at the expense of much of the world's poverty. Since a large percentage of our economy's wealth comes from the production of that which destroys life— weapons, tobacco, alcohol, unhealthy foods, environmentally damaging products and practices—the failure to gain all that we can as participants in God's attempts to secure wholeness for creation is a collective sin. Gaining all that we can as stewards who seek to share in God's creative and redeeming action in the world is an expression of the Bible and Wesley's understanding of stewardship.

Save all you can is the second principle of Wesley's stewardship. "Having gained all you can, by honest wisdom and unwearied diligence . . . *Save all you can*," said Wesley.[4] Again, Wesley's emphasis is a challenge to the contemporary practice of accumulating and hoarding rather than an endorsement of the practice. Wesley was not calling for "the people called Methodists" to invest wisely and build large savings accounts. In fact, he went so far as to compare such practices to "throwing your money into the sea."[5]

"Saving all you can" is Wesley's call to a simplified life-style. It is a warning against extravagance, opulence, and self-gratification. Wesley's list of superfluous expenses would indict most of us. Expensive furniture, clothing, entertainment, unnecessary foods and books, and "elegant gardens" are among his list of unnecessary expenditures. He simply could not reconcile the acquiring of luxuries with the needs of the poor for necessities. Wesley observed that luxuries tend to be viewed as necessities, and that a growing gulf develops between the rich and the poor.

> *"Perhaps the greatest challenge to contemporary western Christians is the willingness to simplify our living. . . ."*

We all know from experience the validity of Wesley's observation. *Things* have a way of increasing in importance. They get into our souls and become a part of our identities. We become dependent on what we own. Where our treasure is, there our heart is also. Soon our possessions own us.

Many of us remember days of scarcity. It is hard to imagine living without color televisions, VCRs, microwave ovens, computerized telephones, and precooked food. Our affluent life-style now is viewed as the necessary norm. With this increased affluence has come an insensitivity and judgmentalism toward those who lack even the necessities. "It's their own fault," we say. Our affluence enables us to live in our suburban ghettos and to avoid even coming into contact with those who struggle to survive in the decaying ghettos of the inner city or the remote mountains.

A contemporary proverb echoes Wesley's challenge to save all you can: live simply so that others may simply live. Perhaps the greatest challenge to contemporary western Christians is the willingness to simplify our living as a counteraction to extravagant living which robs others of the basic necessities of food, shelter, and medical care. When more money is spent on entertainment than on education, on diet products than on food for the hungry, on cosmetics than on dental care for the poor, and on luxury automobiles than on housing for the homeless, a potentially fatal crack has appeared in our ethical and religious foundation. We would do well to heed Wesley's charge to save all we can and to hear Jesus' warning that we must give an account of our stewardship.

The third rule of stewardship, however, gives meaning to the first two. We are to gain all we can and save all we can so that we can *give all we can*. Hear Wesley's own words: "*Save all you can*, by cutting off every expense which serves only to indulge foolish desire, to gratify either the desire of the flesh, the desire of the eye, or the pride of life. Waste nothing . . . on sin or folly, whether for yourself or your children. And then, *give all you can*, or in other words give all you have to God."[6]

Wesley practiced what he preached. As a student, Wesley lived on twenty-eight pounds. He earned thirty pounds, so he gave away two pounds. As his earnings increased, he continued to live on the same twenty-eight pounds. When he earned 120 pounds, he gave away ninety-two pounds. Wesley wrote to his sister, "Money never stays with me. It would burn me if it did. I throw it out of my hands as soon as possible, lest it should find its way into my heart."[7] He told the people that if at his death he had more than ten pounds in his possession, they could call him a robber.[8]

> "If the Methodists would give all they can, then all would have enough."

Wesley's admonition to give was no pious rhetoric designed to increase contributions to the church's budget. It was a plea for generosity rooted in gratitude for God's generosity and a plea for compassion for the poor and needy. He contended that no member of the Methodist Societies should be hungry or poorly housed or inadequately clothed. If the Methodists would give all they can, then all would have enough.

Luke's parable of the steward provided the basis of at least twenty-seven of Wesley's oral sermons delivered between 1741 and 1758. To Wesley, the basic point of the parable is that God holds us accountable for our stewardship and that accountability is based on investing in the lives of others.

In a letter written in A.D. 400, St. Jerome referred to one who "preferred to store her money in the stomachs of the needy rather than to hide it in a purse." That is authentic stewardship! That is savings that matter! That is the righteous use of mammon!

Stewardship—indeed, *discipleship*—is giving one's all in grateful response to God's gracious action on behalf of the world. Extravagance and opulence justified by "I can afford it" is a gross rationalization. Wesley was right in asking, "Can any steward 'afford' to lay out his master's money any other wise than his master appoints him?"[9]

Life belongs to God, who calls us to be caretakers and stewards of creation. Creation exists as God's gift—not to a privileged few, but to all. Proper exercise of stewardship requires the sharing of the earth's resources with all members of God's family.

Wesley's words serve as a fitting conclusion:

> It [money] is an excellent gift of God, answering the noblest ends. In the hands of his children it is food for the hungry, drink for the thirsty, raiment for the naked. It gives to the traveller and the stranger where to lay his head. By it we may supply the place of an husband to the widow, and of a father to the fatherless; we may be a defence for the oppressed, a means of health to the sick, of ease to them that are in pain. It may be as eyes to the blind, as feet to the lame; yea, a lifter up from the gates of death.[10]

Being two-thirds Wesleyan is not being Wesleyan at all. Only by gaining all we can, saving all we can, and giving all we can will we be truly Wesleyan and faithful stewards of God's grace!

> *God said to Moses, "I AM WHO I AM." He said further, "Thus you shall say to the Israelites, I AM has sent me to you."*
>
> *(Exodus 3:14, NRSV)*

Exodus 3:1-15; 33:12-23

The God Beyond Our Knowing

Modern Screen ran a series several years ago called "How the Stars Found Faith." In the series, Jane Russell announced: "I love God. And when you get to know Him, you will find He's a Livin' Doll."[1] About that same time, a survey was conducted among college students to gather information about their religious beliefs. One question was, Who or what is God? One student wrote in bold letters, "I wish I knew!"[2]

Both Jane Russell and the anonymous student have their "amen corners." They represent two long-standing and ever-popular attitudes in the church. In one amen corner are those who know God and unhesitatingly share affirmations about this God. In the other amen corner are those who can reply to the question of who or what God is with only, "I don't know." Some would add, "I wish I did"; others would shrug and say, "And I don't care."

> *"Faith . . . is keeping the tension alive between the God we know and the God beyond our knowing."*

Most of us would be uncomfortable in either corner. We can testify that God is known. After all, we have books full of creeds and affirmations that shape us, challenge us, comfort us, inform us, and sometimes confuse us. We can recite them and even understand parts of them. Yet, we have too many unanswered questions in our minds, too many empty places in our souls, and too much uncertainty in our convictions to more than barely whisper the creeds. We realize that this God we know is more than "a living doll" and more than all the creeds and theologies and hymns and liturgies and temples and sanctuaries can contain.

Faith, real faith, is keeping the tension alive between the God we know and the God beyond our knowing. It is the tension between the God who is as real as a guilty conscience calling for forgiveness and the warm embrace of reconciliation and the God who does not answer when we call out in the dark night of our soul. It is the tension between the God who is as real as the beauty and promise of a brilliant dawn and the God who seems to hide the future from us or whisper the divine word for our time in a voice so low that we cannot hear it. It is the tension between our doctrines—revealed in the sacred Scriptures, refined in the fires of history, and forged on the anvil of the church's experience—and our theological explorations—rising out of new frontiers where old answers do not always fit the new questions and where each generation must follow the ever-moving footprints of the Transcendent One.

This tension is not unlike the tension that Moses felt. Moses met God in the flaming bush. He met a God who knew the sufferings of the people groaning under the yoke of Egyptian slavery. This freedom-loving, slavery-despising God had a plan. The slaves were going to be free. They were going to be given a new future, a promised land. Moses knew God, but Moses wanted to know more. He wanted to be able to get his mind *around* God, so that when the Pharaoh and the people raised questions about who this Liberator was, he could give a definitive answer. Moses wanted to know the Liberator's *name*. "Give me your name, God," Moses said. This God whom Moses knew gave him a name. It didn't help much. God said, "Just tell them 'I AM' sent you." This disturber of Moses' conscience, this emancipator of the oppressed, said, "I AM WHO I AM." In other words, "Moses, I am more than any name can fit."

This "I AM" and Moses formed a close relationship built upon God's promise and Moses' pursuit of it. If ever anyone deserved to see the totality of the Transcendent One, it was Moses. He got close, as close as one could get. Hiding in a cleft of a rock, shielded from the blinding brilliance of the Divine, Moses got only a fleeting peek at the Liberating One's back. This God moves so quickly that at best we catch a glimpse of a light going that way—toward the future.

The people sang the praises of this God who rescued them from the Pharaoh and led them through the waters toward their new tomorrow. But they weren't satisfied with a God that kept moving beyond their grasp, a God who couldn't fit into an easily pronounced, *real* name. Who could hold onto belief in an "I AM"? Who could follow for very long a God who insists on moving before them in a cloud, a God who shows up in a mist, of all things?

> *"No god that can be fashioned totally in an image of gold or in a creed of eloquence is big enough to be the real God. . . ."*

These people got tired of an illusive God. So, they fashioned gods that they could see, touch, define, and actually carry. Faith became allegiance to a fixed god whom they could see clearly, carry easily, and describe minutely—a god with a real name, not a riddle for a name. Were it not for Moses, their act of idolatry would have cost them their future. No completely known god, no god with a restrictive name, could get them to the Promised Land. No god that can be fashioned totally in an image of gold or in a creed of eloquence is big enough to be the real God, the God of the new heaven and the new earth.

Jacob learned this. This God, whom we meet and know, will not be captured by a clever mental hammerlock. If we dare to wrestle this Mysterious One, we may go away with a new name, but we'll go away limping. You can count on that.

Job learned it, too. He thought he had God all figured out. His understanding of God was in the creeds recited glibly by his God-fearing friends. Job was sure that God would fit into his thoughts and arguments. In fact, he was so confident of the airtight logic of his understandings of life and God that he challenged God to a debate. What Job got, however, was a mysterious whirlwind and a deepened trust in One whom he knew but who was beyond his knowing.

The tension between knowing and not knowing is tough to live with. Faith that sustains the tension between the God we know and the God beyond our knowing tempts us to go after other gods or to settle for no god. It makes us want to reduce God to a memorized creed and a firmly defined set of doctrines. "Tell us what we believe," we say to our preacher or to the General Conference.

Just as some people resolve the tension by worshiping golden calves or eloquent creeds or infallible books, so also others opt for either no god or an impersonal mystery—or, as one individual said, "an oblong blur." Some may be intellectuals, whose god is a philosophical system that allows for no transcendent mystery or divine revelation. Some may be functional atheists. Functional atheists are those who believe in the existence of God in the same way that they believe in the reality of unknown planets: they may be real but they are irrelevant to their lives. They might say, "Don't give us any creeds or doctrines. Just give us some fuzzy guidelines and exciting programs and functioning structures. Leave the doctrines and theologies to the professors." That's one way to remove faith's tension.

> *"No affirmations can exhaust the truth of God, and no experience can contain the fullness of God's love and grace."*

Authentic faith affirms that God is both known and beyond our knowing. It celebrates the God who is revealed in creation, who works in history, who was incarnate in Jesus Christ, and who is a presence in the community of faith. God is known in our creeds, our liturgies, our affirmations, and our experiences. But this same God also is more than has been revealed, or more than we have known. No creeds can exhaust God's reality, no liturgies can adequately worship this Holy One, no affirmations can exhaust the truth of God, and no experience can contain the fullness of God's love and grace.

I have lived most of my life within clear view of mountains. They were part of my experience long before I knew what they were or even noticed that they were there. In fact, it was only after I left them for a while and lived where no mountains could be seen that I really came to realize how much mountains were a part of my life.

There is much about the mountains that I know and love: their majestic peaks which stretch to grasp the sky; their seasonal change of clothes from the pure white garments of winter to the young, cheerful blooms and buds of spring. I love when the deep greens accented with laurel corsages clothe them in summer, and when a resourceful artist covers the mountains with the multicolored canvas of autumn. The mountains give birth to the cool streams and launch them on their way to the mighty oceans. The mountains are filled with symphonic sounds. Some birds, like the crow, always sing off pitch and insist on a solo part; other birds are more like a choir accompanied by an orchestra of insects. The symphony is interrupted by the wind in the trees or by the questioning of an owl. The mountains are full of life. Towering fir trees and giant oaks spread their arms so that the birds may perch on them and sing their melodies. There the birds build their nests, hatch their little ones, and send them into flight. Bears sleep in their hollow trunks, and squirrels play in their branches.

I know that mountains are beautiful, majestic, awesome. I have seen their splendor and beauty from many a front porch and from the vantage point of a lofty peak. I have heard their sounds, smelled their fragrances, drank from their springs, and followed their trails. I have felt their cool breezes and have rested in their refreshing shade. I know the mountains! They are my place of birth. They are my home. They are part of me.

But I don't really know the mountains. I can't get my eyes

around, over, and under them. My ears cannot absorb their endless sounds. My feet cannot traverse their grueling trails. My senses cannot receive fully their sights, their tastes, their fragrances, or their textures. I do know enough about them, however, to be moved to sing with the Psalmist, "I will lift up my eyes to the hills, from whence cometh my help" (Psalm 121:1, KJV). I know enough about the mountains to know that before them I am a small, finite, temporary creature. I have experienced enough of their reality that I want to see more of their beauty, hear more of their music, taste more of their fruits, smell more of their perfume, feel more of their life, and explore more of their unmarked trails.

"Before the mountains were brought forth . . . from everlasting to everlasting you are God" (Psalm 90:2, NRSV)—one whom we know but who is beyond our knowing. As people of faith, we celebrate the God we know and we ever explore the unchartered paths of a God who is beyond our knowing.

In a sermon entitled "On the Omnipresence of God," John Wesley celebrated the knowable God. But in that same sermon he recited a verse from a hymn written by Samuel Wesley:

> Hail, Father! whose creating call,
> Unnumbered worlds attend!
> Jehovah, comprehending all,
> Whom none can comprehend![3]

John 17:11b-21

United by a Shared Faith

In a sermon preached in London on November 24, 1765, John Wesley said the following:

> How dreadful and how innumerable are the contests which have arisen about religion! And not only among the children of this world, among those who knew not what true religion was; but even among the children of God, those who had experienced 'the kingdom of God within them'. . . . How many of these in all ages, instead of joining together against the common enemy, have turned their weapons against each other, and so not only wasted their precious time but hurt one another's spirits, weakened each other's hands, and so hindered the great work of their common Master! . . . How many of the 'lame turned out of the way'! How many sinners confirmed in their disregard of all religion, and their contempt of those that profess it![1]

We are all embarrassed to read the headlines reporting conflict between Protestants and Catholics, between Christians and Hindus, between Jews and Moslems, and even between Christians and other Christians. How far we are from the fulfillment of our Lord's vision in the prayer he prayed a few hours before his death! He prayed, "So that they may be one, as we are one" (John 17:11, NRSV). If God is one and Christ and God are one, then the church also must be one—not one in organization or structure, nor in uniformity of belief or

82

commonality of worship, but one in spirit and in a common loyalty to Christ.

In a letter to Mrs. Howton dated October 3, 1783, John Wesley declared, "It is the glory of the people called Methodists that they condemn none for their opinions or modes of worship. They think and let think."[2] A basic motto of our Wesleyan heritage is this: In essentials, unity; in nonessentials, freedom; and in all things, charity.[3] Therein lies an avenue to the oneness for which Christ prayed.

> *"United Methodists affirm a core of Christian beliefs that other churches share."*

In essentials, unity. Although there may be varied interpretations of the essentials, United Methodists affirm a core of Christian beliefs that other churches share. Permit me to share a quick overview of these basic affirmations.

One affirmation is belief in the triune God. Individual churches may differ in their understanding of the Trinity, but we Methodists share a common belief that God is known in three basic categories. We know God as Creator/Father, the one who brings creation into being and sustains life. God can be and is known in the created order. The beauty, intricacy, vastness, and splendor of this magnificent universe reveal God as Father.

But God is more than nature reveals, and God's presence and purposes go beyond creating and sustaining the universe. God is known in the historical Jesus, who was born, who lived among us, and who was crucified and raised from the dead. Jesus the Christ is the revelation of God and God's purpose for human life. Jesus is all of God that can be revealed in a human being. That does not mean that Jesus is all there is of God. He is all of God that can be contained in human form. We meet the living God in Jesus of Nazareth!

God is still more, however, than is expressed in creation and in the historical Jesus. God is not limited to "out there" in the created order, or to "back there" in the historical Jesus. God is *within* persons and communities as one who comforts, sustains, reconciles, forgives, and guides. God is the Holy Spirit, a presence known in life's ups and downs—life's joys and sorrows.

We affirm with our Christian brothers and sisters our faith in the triune God—Father, Son, and Holy Spirit—who creates, redeems, and sustains. We also affirm salvation in and through Jesus Christ. God has acted mysteriously and decisively in the life, teaching, death, and resurrection of Jesus the Christ to bring salvation, wholeness, and peace to all creation. "In Christ God was reconciling the world to himself" (II Cor. 5:19, NRSV). In Christ, God has identified with the human lot—God has experienced its pain and joy, its struggle and serenity, its sin and brokenness. In Christ we experience forgiveness, healing, and reconciliation with our true selves, with others, and with God.

And it is all a gift! Our identity as daughters and sons of God, our reconciliation and forgiveness, our hope and purposes are free gifts of God. They are *grace*. Our worth is purely God's claim upon *us*—not upon our achievements, our knowledge, or even our goodness or beliefs. "For by grace you have been saved through faith, and this is not your own doing; it is the gift of God" (Eph. 2:8, NRSV). We share this basic affirmation with Baptists and Lutherans, Catholics and Presbyterians, and Disciples and Episcopalians.

Furthermore, we affirm the essential oneness and universality of the church. We claim the whole church—with its diversity of gifts and its interdependency—as the body of Christ. No denomination is the total body of Christ. Each community of faith has its unique heritage and its distinctive emphases. No part of this body can claim sovereignty or superiority. All are united in a common commitment to the lordship of Christ, who is capable of blending our diverse gifts into a symphony of praise to God.

We United Methodists, along with other Christians, find hope in the present and future reign of God. What God began in creation and what God revealed in Christ Jesus, God will bring to completion. God is sovereign. God's kingdom is in our midst whenever and wherever the purposes of God are fulfilled. Yet, we know only intimations of God's victory. God's vision for the world will become reality. Wherever we see that vision lived out, God's reign is present. We live toward "a new heaven and a new earth; . . . [where God] will wipe every tear from their eyes [and where] death will be no more" (Rev. 21:1, 3, NRSV); where "the leopard shall lie down with the kid, the calf and the lion and the fatling together, and a little child shall lead them" (Isa. 11:6, NRSV); and where nations "shall beat their swords into plowshares, and their spears into pruning hooks; nation shall not lift up sword against nation, neither shall they learn war any more" (Isa. 2:4, NRSV). This we believe! This we trust! This we live toward!

Another essential that we United Methodists share with other Christians is belief in the authority of the Bible. We may differ as to the source or meaning of the Bible's authority. Some find the Bible's authority in its inerrancy, its factual accuracy. Others root the Bible's authority in the validity and power of the Word beneath the words, in the living God to whom the Bible bears witness. Together, however, we take the Bible seriously. It is authoritative in matters of faith as God speaks the Divine Word in human language.

In essentials, unity! Triune God, salvation in and through Jesus Christ as a gift of God's grace, the oneness of the church, the present and future reign of God, the authority of Scripture— these are threads that run through the tapestry of Christendom.

> *"In responding to the great 'I AM WHO I AM,' we must allow for freedom."*

In nonessentials, freedom. What are *nonessentials*? For Wesley, nonessentials included such things as forms of worship, modes of baptism, and church polity. The specific language and images of the core doctrines that we have just shared are among the nonessentials. The reality of a God who creates, sustains, redeems, reconciles, and brings to fulfillment the divine purposes is the heart of religion—not the language or symbols of the reality. We can construct idols from language as surely as from gold. The precise formulation and interpretations of the marrow of belief must not be our golden calf—a substitute for the God who transcends the languages of all peoples; a God whose likeness cannot be clearly fashioned by the works of our hands, the constraints of our minds, or the images of our speech.

In responding to the great "I AM WHO I AM," we must allow for freedom. We think and let think. We enter into dialogue with others in a spirit of humility, knowing that God is not without witness among any peoples.

In essentials, unity; in nonessentials, freedom; in all things charity. Ah, now we are getting to the real core of religion. In his sermon "The Unity of the Divine Being," John Wesley said, "True religion is right tempers towards God and man. It is, in two words, gratitude and benevolence: gratitude to our Creator and supreme Benefactor, and benevolence to our fellow-creatures. In other words, it is the loving God with all our heart, and our neighbour as ourselves."[4] Likewise, Wesley's famous sermon "Catholic Spirit" is based on II Kings 10:15. Jehu greets Jehonadab with the question, "Is thine heart right, as my heart is with thy heart? . . . If it be, give me thine hand" (KJV). Wesley's sermon calls the church to a spirit of oneness centered in love for God and neighbor as commanded by Christ.

> *"In our Wesleyan tradition, rejection and hatred in the name of faithfulness to creeds are but pious sins."*

How often we religious folk throw the heart of religion out the window in arguments over religion. We all know persons who refuse to associate with members of their own families because of disagreements over interpretations of the Bible, or modes of baptism, or some other theological formulation. A family in a church I served many years ago walked out of worship when I referred to the book of Jonah as a sermon on God's universal mercy rather than a historical account of a man's journey into the belly of a fish. The family refused to speak to me thereafter because, in their words, "He doesn't believe the Bible."

Gore Vidal's novel *Julian* comments upon the hypocrisy of religion's failure to be charitable in all things. One day young Julian, who was to be emperor, was walking through the streets when he saw a commotion. When he went to see what was going on, he saw some monks viciously beating two old men whom they called heretics. The old men and the monks were arguing over the doctrine of the Trinity. As a monk cocked his arm to deliver another blow, he shouted, "Misguided fools who believe that Jesus and God are exactly the same . . . " As young Julian watched this violence in the name of religion, he thought, "A religion of brotherhood and mildness which daily murders those who disagree with its doctrines can only be thought hypocrite, or worse."[5]

Wesley was right to refer to the practice of substituting doctrines and beliefs for the practice of love as *religious bigotry*. In our Wesleyan tradition, rejection and hatred in the name of faithfulness to creeds are but pious sins.

The God in whom we believe and whom we trust is love. God's love knows no boundaries of race, or class, or nation, or creed. As those called to be the people of God who reflect the divine image, our love includes those with whom we may disagree on matters of doctrine. It is, after all, by our love that they shall know we are Christians, not by our uniformity of creedal statements. We are the body of Christ. Christ's body was broken *for* us. May it not be broken *by* us.

In all things, charity! We live in a fractured and divided world. Religion contributes to the division and hostility among the world's people. What God intends to be a means of uniting the human family too frequently becomes a source of enmity, competition, and outright warfare.

Faith, however, can unite us. Faith centers in God, the Creator who comes to reconcile and redeem, to empower and sustain; who through the Bible and an inspiring Presence in a covenantal community ever moves the world toward a new heaven and a new earth in which the prayer of the Christ is answered: "So that they might be one, as we are one" (John 17:11, NRSV).

In essentials, unity; in nonessentials, freedom; in all things, love.

Notes

The Church's Search for Identity

1. Albert C. Outler, ed., *The Works of John Wesley* (Nashville: Abingdon Press, 1986), vol. 3, p. 46.
2. Ibid., 1987, vol. 4, pp. 85f.
3. Ibid., 1986, vol. 3, p. 56-57.

Nourished by Our Roots

1. Colin W. Williams, *John Wesley's Theology Today* (Nashville: Abingdon Press, 1960), pp. 28-29.
2. "Events and People: Campbell on the SBC," *The Christian Century,* November 5, 1986, p. 969.

Balancing Beliefs and Behavior

1. Outler, *The Works of John Wesley,* 1987, vol. 4, p. 90.

The Tough Mind and the Tender Heart

1. *The Methodist Hymnal* (Nashville: The Methodist Publishing House, 1964), p. 344.
2. *The Works of John Wesley,* 3rd ed. (Grand Rapids: Baker Book House, 1979), vol. 8, pp. 314-15.
3. Outler, *The Works of John Wesley,* 1979, vol. 1, p. 176.
4. Ibid., 1985, vol. 2, p. 599.
5. Ibid., p. 600.
6. *The Methodist Hymnal,* p. 344.

Tools for the Task

1. "John Wesley and The Wholeness of Scripture," *Interpretation,* July 1985, p. 251.

Transforming Grace

1. *The Works of John Wesley,* 3rd ed. (Grand Rapids: Baker Book House, 1979), vol. 1, p. 103.
2. Paul Tournier, *The Meaning of Gifts* (John Knox Press, 1964), p. 59.

Going on to Perfection

1. *The Book of Discipline of The United Methodist Church* (Nashville: The United Methodist Publishing House, 1988), p. 232.
2. Outler, *The Works of John Wesley,* 1986, vol. 3, p. 75, footnote 29.
3. John Telford, ed., *The Letters of John Wesley* (London: The Epworth Press, 1931), vol. 8, p. 238.
4. *The Works of John Wesley,* 3rd ed. (Grand Rapids: Baker Book House, 1979), vol. 13, p. 105.
5. Nehemiah Curnock, ed., *The Journal of John Wesley,* standard ed. (London: Epworth Press, 1938), vol. 4, p. 529.
6. Outler, *The Works of John Wesley,* 1986, vol. 3, p. 75.
7. Ibid., 1984, vol. 1, p. 403.
8. Ibid., 1986, vol. 3, p. 74.
9. Harry Emerson Fosdick, *The Man from Nazareth* (New York: Harper and Row, 1949), p. 106.
10. Orlo Strunk, Jr., *In Faith and Love* (Nashville: Graded Press, 1968), pp. 15-27.
11. Ibid., p. 19.
12. Outler, *The Works of John Wesley,* 1985, vol. 2, pp. 122, 124.

Being Saved Isn't Enough

1. Gerald Kennedy, *The Methodist Way of Life* (Englewood Clifts: Prentice-Hall, Inc., 1958), p. 193.
2. *The Book of Discipline,* p. 45.

On Being Two-Thirds Wesleyan

1. Outler, *The Works of John Wesley,* 1987, vol. 4, p. 91.
2. Ibid., p. 96.
3. Ibid., p. 95.
4. Ibid., 1985, vol. 2, p. 273.
5. Ibid., p. 276.
6. Ibid., p. 279.

7. Lovett Hayes Weems, *The Gospel According to Wesley* (Nashville: Discipleship Resources, 1982), p. 49.
8. Ibid.
9. Outler, *The Works of John Wesley,* 1987, vol. 4, p. 92.
10. Ibid., 1985, vol. 2, p. 268.

The God Beyond Our Knowing

1. Eric F. Goldman, *The Crucial Decade—And After: America, 1945-1960* (New York: Vintage Books, 1961), p. 305.
2. G. Ernest Thomas, *How To Live Your Faith* (New York: Fleming H. Revell Company, 1958), p. 11.
3. Outler, *The Works of John Wesley,* 1987, vol. 4, p. 42.

United by a Shared Faith

1. Outler, *The Works of John Wesley,* 1984, vol. 1, p. 449.
2. Ibid., p. 87, footnote 77.
3. Ibid., 1985, vol. 2, pp. 81-95. [Wesley's sermon, "Catholic Spirit," gives a summary of this emphasis.]
4. Ibid., 1987, vol. 4, pp. 66-67.
5. Gore Vidal, *Julian* (Boston: Little, Brown, & Co., 1964), p. 31.

Resources for Further Study

The following are helpful sources for doctrinal preaching.

Abbey, Merrill R. *Living Doctrine in a Vital Pulpit*. Nashville: Abingdon Press, 1964. An older but helpful book in defining doctrinal preaching and its relationship to life.

Cushman, Robert E. *John Wesley's Experimental Divinity*. Decatur, GA: Kingswood Books, 1989. Insightful essays on key elements of Wesley's theology.

Langford, Thomas A. *Practical Divinity: Theology in The Wesleyan Tradition*. Nashville: Abingdon Press, 1983. A historical survey of theological figures and themes from Wesley up to the late twentieth century.

Langford, Thomas A. and Patricia B. Jelinek. *Grace Upon Grace*. Nashville: Graded Press, 1990. A five-session study of the mission statement adopted by the 1988 General Conference.

Madsen, Norman. *This We Believe*. Nashville: Graded Press, 1987. A study of the Articles of Religion of the United Methodist Church.

McKim, Donald K. *Theological Turning Points*. Louisville: John Knox Press, 1988. Provides a historical development of eight Christian doctrines.

Outler, Albert C., ed. *The Works of John Wesley, Vol. 1-4*. Nashville: Abingdon Press, 1984-87. Comprehensive source books which include helpful introductions and notes by a noted Wesley scholar.

Stokes, Mack B. *Major United Methodist Beliefs*. Nashville: Abingdon Press, 1990. A helpful guide to distinctly United Methodist beliefs and those of other Wesleyan denominations.

Sugden, Edward H., ed. *John Wesley's Fifty-Three Sermons*. Nashville: Abingdon Press, 1983. A sampling of Wesley's most famous sermons.

Wallace, Horace L. and Lewis V. Baldwin. *Touched By Grace: Black Methodist Heritage in The United Methodist Church*. Nashville: Graded Press, 1986. A thirteen-session study resource that traces key figures and themes from Wesley's time up through today.

Williams, Colin W. *John Wesley's Theology Today*. Nashville: Abingdon Press, 1960. Helpful treatment of Wesley's basic understanding of grace, perfection, assurance, holiness, and other beliefs.